THE ART
of STENCILING

MARY HICKEY

Martingale
& COMPANY

BOTHELL, WASHINGTON

ACKNOWLEDGMENT AND DEDICATION

Few people would have the patience and kindness of my husband, Phil,
who helps in every way imaginable with endless good-natured generosity.

Martingale & Company
PO Box 118
Bothell, WA 98041-0118
www.patchwork.com

Pastimes is an imprint of Martingale & Company.

Printed in China.
05 04 03 02 01 00 8 7 6 5 4 3 2 1

Library of Congress Cataloging-in-Publication Data

Hickey, Mary
    The art of stenciling / Mary Hickey.
       p. cm.
    ISBN 1-56477-304-3
    1. Stencil work.   I. Title.

TT270.H623 2000
745.7'3—dc21

                00-026001

MISSION STATEMENT

We are dedicated to providing quality products
and service by working together to inspire creativity
and to enrich the lives we touch.

CREDITS

President · Nancy J. Martin
CEO · Daniel J. Martin
Publisher · Jane Hamada
Editorial Director · Mary V. Green
Design and Production Manager · Stan Green
Cover Designer · Stan Green
Text Designer · Trina Stahl
Technical Editor · Dawn Anderson
Copy Editor · Karen Koll
Illustrator · Robin Strobel
Photographer · Brent Kane

CONTENTS

PREFACE

IN 1936, IN the depths of the depression, my father wanted to give my mother a wonderful gift as a wedding present. He had no money, but a friend gave him several large pieces of walnut. With these chunks of wood, he used his architect's eye and artist's hands to design and build a bed. Using a borrowed lathe and saw, he hand-shaped four tall posts and a headboard and footboard. With sandpaper, stain, and wax he burnished the wood until it glowed a deep rich brown. The elegantly simple bed was exquisitely designed and beautifully shaped. This bed was indeed a wonderful wedding present, and over the years it became a symbol to me of my father's ingenuity and creativity. For his seventieth birthday, I made an elaborate "Mariner's Compass" quilt for him to use on the bed. Around this same time, I began to dream of owning the bed. However, as a middle child, I knew it would never be mine. I knew that by rights it should go to my older brother. Slowly, quietly, my desire for the bed started to grow and fester. When I realized that I would be foolish to let the bed harm my relationship with my siblings, I decided to find a way to appease my desire for the walnut bed.

I cut several large stencils, bought some taupe and brown paint, and painted a shadow, two posts, and a headboard on our bedroom wall. The result appeared to be a lovely old walnut bed. My husband loved this stenciled bed because he didn't have to crawl around like an acrobat to plug in our lamps. Our children thought it was great fun to fool their friends with it.

The walnut bed marked the beginning of my stenciling career. For a while, no surface was safe in our house. I looked at every wall, each piece of furniture, and even windows, envisioning stenciling designs on them. Fortunately other people started hiring me to decorate their homes, so my passion for stenciling has had a long and happy history. In this book, you will see that stenciling is a remarkably simple craft and that this simplicity is the hallmark of fine design.

Years later, when my brother and I were cleaning out our father's house, I washed and folded the "Mariner's Compass" quilt I had given to my father, and insisted that my brother take the quilt for the walnut bed. My brother said that he would treasure the quilt but that I was to have the bed!

Stenciled headboard and posts look almost as real as the original walnut headboard made by my father.

INTRODUCTION

STENCILING IS INSTANTLY rewarding. Since you decide what design to use, which colors to paint, and where to place them, stenciling allows you to make your own unique mark on your surroundings.

Stencils can be used on large or small projects, walls, fabrics, floors or furniture. Think of all the times you have found a pattern you liked, but the colors were wrong. With stenciling you can customize the colors for your own individual look. I particularly like the soft, dimensional quality of painted patterns, eliminating the "dead" feeling that wallpapers so often have.

Choose your stencil motif and its colors to echo the elements in your room—fabrics, paintings, and furniture. For example, a few leaves stenciled along one corner of a picture frame could come from the picture itself or from elsewhere in the room. A motif stenciled on the walls or furniture could be adapted to brighten a tablecloth, curtain, or duvet cover. This continuity is one of the marks of good design.

In the project section of the book, you will see photographs of stenciling in many rooms and on various surfaces, including paper, wood, and fabric. The projects show stencils used either singly or as repeats. The first project, a small chest, teaches the basics of stenciling and is a good beginner project.

Most of the stencil designs shown

This elegant little basket quilt is stenciled directly on the living room wall. Many of the shapes were stenciled through pieces of window and fence screening to produce the look of checked fabric. Hundreds of pencil dots smudged by my thumb create the soft look of intricate quilting.

in the photographs are printed on the pages of the book for you to trace. Use the motifs as shown or reduce or enlarge them on a photocopy machine. Feel free to adapt the stencils by adding or changing shapes to coordinate with other elements in your decorating scheme.

Several of the stencils mix easily with other stencils. For example, look at the ivy swag on page 91. Stencil the existing swag around the upper part of a room. Or, enhance the swag by adding the birds as shown on page 57. If you prefer, add the bird nest and eggs or birds in nest on page 91.

Stenciling is simple, speedy, and stunning. It is a lovely method of adding charm and individuality to your home. So try it and have fun.

Supplies

A STENCIL IS simply a pattern of holes in a piece of paper or plastic. You apply paint to an object through the holes. The stencil consists of holes or windows and a series of little bridges. The bridges help hold the stencil together and are also an important part of the design. In a well-designed stencil, the bridges and windows give a fluid, rhythmic quality to the design. The bridges often occur where one shape passes behind another, creating depth in the design. To get started making and using stencils, you need a few supplies.

Photocopy Machines If you want to change the size of a stencil, trace the design on paper and take it to a copy center. Use the reduction or enlargement feature, setting it to the percentage of change you want. To greatly enlarge a design you may have to work in several stages or in several sections, jigsaw-puzzle style.

Stencil Materials To make stencils from the designs in this book or from your own designs, use lightweight (.005 millimeter) sheets of acetate, available in large sheets or in a tablet from art-supply stores. Lightweight acetate is stiff enough to hold its shape yet thin enough to be cut easily with a craft knife. Since it is transparent, tracing the design is easy. Keep in mind that on a photocopy machine you can copy your

designs directly onto the acetate, eliminating the tracing step.

If acetate is unavailable, cut the stencils from card-stock paper (manila folders work well). After cutting the stencil, coat both sides of the paper with polyurethane to seal it. This coating will keep the moisture in the paint from damaging the paper.

Most stencil artists prefer a .005 weight of acetate. Acetate can be clear or etched.

Tracing Pens Use a permanent felt-tip marker (such as a Sanford Sharpie) or a technical drawing pen (such as a Pilot ultra-fine-point permanent pen) to trace the design on the acetate. Look for a pen that will bond and not smear on the acetate.

Look for black or blue pens with ink that will stick to acetate.

Cutting Tools X-Acto, Olfa, Excel, and Dexter all make excellent knives for cutting the windows in your stencil. Use a knife with a long, sharp-tipped blade. The secret to making stencils easily is to buy extra blades and change them as often as necessary. On long straight lines and gentle curves use a small rotary cutter. In a pinch you can use a carpenter's utility knife with a new blade.

Use a very sharp tip on your knife.

Electric tools called "stencil burners" work remarkably well for cutting stencils. They have a fine tip that is heated to melt lines in the acetate, in effect cutting the stencil without the need for pressure. Available at art-supply and craft stores, stencil burners range in price from $25 to $35 and are well worth the cost if you intend to do several projects.

A stencil burner will make cutting stencils from acetate quick and effortless.

Paper Punches and Specialty Scissors The recent revival of scrapbooks and memory books has led to the production of many interesting paper hole punches. Consider the simplicity of punching a series of large and small holes and hearts to create the lacy effect of eyelet or doilies. Other punches such as a daisy, a maple leaf, and a scroll enable you to cut really intricate designs easily. Scalloped and zigzag scissors blades make it easy to cut stencils with interesting edges.

Paper punches and specialty scissors are available in a variety of designs and readily cut through acetate.

Removable Tape Keep a roll of removable tape, such as painter's (blue) masking tape, with your stenciling tools. Use it to help hold the stencil in place without damaging the surface you are painting. Carefully placed tape functions, in many projects, as a stencil itself.

Glue Sticks (Removable Formula) Glue sticks now come in a removable formula that works very nicely. Simply spread a thin coat on the back of the stencil. This will hold up for five or six moves.

Repositionable Spray Adhesive Art-supply and craft stores sell repositionable spray adhesive. After cutting your stencil, spray the back lightly with repositionable spray adhesive and allow three to five minutes for the adhesive to "dry." The adhesive will still be very sticky but will "let go" of the wall or surface when you have painted the section. The adhesive will form a close bond with the painted surface and prevent the paint from seeping under the stencil while you work. When you are finished painting a motif, gently peel the stencil directly away from the surface to avoid smudging, and reposition it. Acrylic paints, sparingly applied, will dry immediately. This will allow you to paint and move your stencil several times before you have to spray with adhesive again. If you cannot find repositionable spray, go ahead and buy any spray adhesive you can find. Just spritz the back of the stencil very lightly and allow about ten minutes for the stencil to "dry" before placing it on your wall or work surface.

These adhesives hold the stencil in place, and then release it undamaged.

Palette Use a paint palette as a surface for mixing your stencil paints. Your palette can be a paper plate, a saucer, a soap dish, or (my favorite) an ice cube tray.

Bottle and Jar Paints The secret to painting stencils with any kind of paint lies in having only tiny amounts of paint on your brush and using a pouncing or dabbing motion with the brush held vertically against the stencil. The overall effect should be just a mist of color on the object to be decorated. Paints sold in bottles or jars formulated specifically for stenciling are thick, dry very quickly, and provide the desirable subtle haze-like quality. However, by using only small amounts of paint and pouncing the brush on a paper towel first, you can use almost any type of paint.

Pounce the paint on the brush onto a paper towel until only a fine mist of paint shows up.

Allow the paint colors to mist over other colors to create a soft watercolor effect.

Stencil Crayons Craft stores often sell stencil paints in a crayon form. Rub the crayon color onto a saucer or disposable container. Pick up the paint with your brush, using a brisk circular motion. Pounce or circle the paint through the stencil windows onto the surface. Stencil crayons provide the same ability to control the process as the liquid paints.

Spray Paints Spray paints are available in a vast range of colors in craft, hardware, and auto-parts stores. These paints dry instantly and are compatible with most surfaces. Spray paints provide a beautiful fine haze of subtle color.

Warning: Safety Precautions
Spray paint can be toxic. Read the manufacturer's instructions on the can. Work in a well-ventilated space away from open flames. Wear an appropriate face mask, goggles, and tight-fitting gloves. Keep spray paints away from babies, children, and pregnant women.

Bristle Brushes The traditional tool for applying stencil paint is a blunt-ended brush with stiff bristles. When stenciling, you apply the paint with an up-and-down or stippling motion vertically through the stencil windows without letting it seep under the edges. To do this, you need specially designed brushes that are tube shaped, with stiff bristles cut straight across at the end. Bristle brushes, available in several sizes, enable you to paint your designs with beautiful subtlety. To start, you may wish to purchase two or more ½" brushes and two or more brushes about 1" in diameter.

If the bristles are very long, an inch or more, the bristles will bend and sneak under the edges of the stencil as you paint, smudging your design. To avoid this problem, try wrapping the bristles with masking tape as shown in the photograph on page 29.

Different applicators will create varied textures.

Foam Brushes Foam brushes in the shape of a small biscuit with a wooden handle work well for large designs in bold colors. Foam brushes are available in several sizes. Choose sizes that are appropriate to the scale of your design.

You will need several brushes for the various light and dark colors you intend to stipple. Tightly wrap the brushes in plastic bags or plastic wrap to prevent the paint from drying during short interruptions in your painting.

Many paint and craft stores sell small foam paint rollers. While it will not produce as sophisticated an effect as a brush, a foam paint roller covers a lot of stenciling without too much work. Just remember to use very little paint and a light touch.

Permanent Marking Pens Artists often "paint" with colored ink or felt-tip pens to create shading, volume, and depth in their work. By dragging an ink pen along the edge of a ruler or stencil, you can quickly create the illusion of depth and dimension.

Outlining the sails with a felt-tip pen adds clarity to the sailboat.

DESIGN SUGGESTIONS

Stencils that are repeated as a pattern should be absorbed into the room and gently enhance the lines and elements of the room rather than dominate the space. Stenciled patterns should influence the character of the room; for example, the placement of the ribbon-and-flower stencil shown on page 30 at just below the center of the wall brings your eye down to the feminine furniture and creates the illusion of a dado or chair rail. Many modern homes lack these architectural details and benefit greatly from a stenciled substitute.

In general, the more geometric the design, the more careful you must be to plan the design to fit exactly into the available space. It is, of course, possible to continue around the room and simply bend the flexible stencil to turn the corner, or to add a fragment of the design, but this often has the irritating properties of a crooked picture. Spend a little time adjusting a pattern to fit into the space exactly; you will be happy you did. You may have to re-space the repeats slightly or cut a special little piece that finishes the design at the end of the room.

Look at the space and decide where the visual center of the room is. See "Centering" on page 11. Take into consideration any large architectural elements—such as a doorway, large window, or fireplace—that create a visual center other than one strictly measured by the exact center. Once you have found the center, decide whether to center the middle of the stencil or the end of the stencil.

Plan from the center toward the corners of the room. Calculate the number of complete pattern repeats that will fit in the allotted space. Then decide how to manage the corners. If, by some bit of good luck, the pattern works out to fit perfectly from corner to corner, count your blessings and start stenciling. However, usually you will have to measure the remaining space and decide how best to fill it gracefully. Swags and garlands require careful thought before stenciling since they are large rhythmic elements that are quite annoying if they are not right. Planning is all the more important, both to avoid cutting off the repeat and to make sure the placement of the design works well with any large piece of furniture in the room. It is easy to adjust the spacing of swags of leaves and garlands of flowers by simply adding or subtracting a few leaves or flowers.

In many houses, the walls are not truly vertical, nor are the ceilings accurately horizontal. A rigidly geometrical border may not be visually pleasing in such a room. Look for more free-flowing or asymmetrical designs to help you camouflage these problems.

I usually take stock of the room with my measuring tape, calculator, and my artistic eye. I plan the general scheme of things and start the project. After painting a few repeats I stop and look at the project. After digesting the impact of the stenciling, I often make changes and adjust my plans. Often I continue on with my original plan, but sometimes I decide that the room does not need any more stenciling and stop.

The ivy border ends in a complete pattern repeat at the end of the wall. A complete ivy motif begins on the adjacent wall just around the corner.

TECHNIQUES

To stencil, you apply paint lightly over the holes, or windows, in a stencil, using an up-and-down motion with the brush. The dabbing motion is called *stippling* or *pouncing*. With this delicate coloring of the motifs, stencils become beautiful, subtle designs, rich in movement. They take on a three-dimensional quality.

USING THE STENCIL DESIGNS IN THIS BOOK

Many stencil designs are included in this book. If the design is already the size you want, simply trace or photocopy the motif onto your chosen stencil material. You can also reduce or enlarge any of the designs on a photocopy machine or add your own touches to them. Feel free to combine several elements in any project. Add some strawberries to the ivy swags, ribbons to the flowers, and birds anywhere.

Many of the stencils in this book have several components. Feel free to mix and match components to create new images. You may be able to use a large, elaborate design on a piece of furniture, but you may wish to use just of few of the components from the same stencil on a coordinating accessory. For example, the oak-leaf table was made with the two stencil designs on page 87. By taking indi-vidual motifs from one of those stencils and combining them in a new way, you can create a coordinating image to stencil on a place mat or napkin.

Not all stenciling has to be done as a border or in a predictable order. For example, birds randomly stenciled around the walls of a room create an open, airy feeling, and a few houses stenciled on a lower wall give a casual, playful atmosphere to a house.

Use a subtle touch to stencil a few light, airy birds along the border in your room.

MAKING YOUR OWN STENCILS

Making your own stencils is as easy as tracing a drawing from a child's coloring book. Think of it as tracing twice, once with a felt-tip pen and a second time with a craft knife.

TRANSFERRING YOUR DESIGN

Whether you trace by hand or use a copy machine, transferring the design to acetate or card-stock paper is the first step in stenciling. To transfer by hand, lay your sheet of acetate or paper over the design and anchor it in place with masking tape. Trace the motif onto acetate with a pen suitable for acetate, such as a Pilot ultra-fine-point permanent pen or Sanford Sharpie. Or transfer the motif to paper with a pencil. For a clearer view of the image through the paper, place the paper and image over a light source, such as a window or light box. If desired, shade in the areas to be cut out. The shading will help you see the pieces that are to be removed.

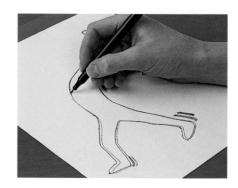

Trace your design onto acetate.

If you need to change the size of your design, you will find it worthwhile to make a trip to a photocopy machine. Use the reducing or enlarging feature on the copy machine to resize the design. Then place clear acetate or card-stock paper in the paper holder of the copy machine and make one or more copies of your newly sized design. If desired, use a felt-tip pen to shade in the areas to be cut out.

CUTTING THE STENCILS

USING a sharp blade in your craft knife and a self-healing cutting mat, cut out the stencil. Cutting mats are available at craft stores and fabric stores. The mats will extend the life of your cutting knife. They come in a variety of sizes and are a worthwhile investment.

Hold the acetate in place on the mat with your spare hand and start at the center of a design. Always pull the knife toward your cutting arm and away from your spare hand. Try to use a fluid movement rather than fast starts and stops. Whenever possible, turn the stencil rather than the knife. You have more control this way. Try to complete each line or curve in a single, long stroke, without raising the blade. This will give you a cleaner line when you paint with the stencil.

Cut the smaller parts of an intricate design before the larger parts. This will insure that the stencil keeps its strength for as long as possible during the cutting process.

Repair cutting mistakes by covering both sides of the acetate with clear tape and recutting the area. If the stencil you want is larger than a single sheet of acetate, join several sheets with tape.

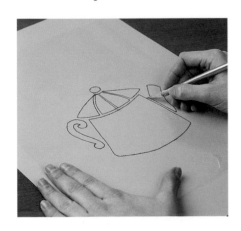

Use a craft knife to cut along the traced lines.

PREPARING SURFACES FOR STENCILING

As with any successful decorating project, the first steps are planning and preparation. Examine the background surface and fill, sand, and paint as necessary. Rather than using paint stripper, I usually clean up old furniture with a kitchen cleanser and sand lightly before painting with a base coat of latex paint. Background paint must be clean and well dried before you begin to stencil so you do not remove any of it when you pull your stencil off for repositioning. For easier stenciling, be sure to remove any knobs or drawer pulls from furniture before painting the base coat. Reattach them when you have finished stenciling.

Look at the surface to be stenciled and establish some mental guidelines for the overall positioning of the design. Your goal is to have the background and the stencil form a single unified whole rather than two elements that fight with each other.

CENTERING

FIND the exact center of a wall by marking the crossing point of two pieces of string stretched diagonally across the surface. Remember though, that if the wall has aspects that are not symmetrical—for example, a doorway to one side—you may prefer to find the visual center of the room instead. Simply find the center from the edge of the door to the corners of the wall.

MARKING VERTICAL OR HORIZONTAL SPACES

To establish vertical lines, hang a plumb line from the top of the wall to the floor. Mark the wall at intervals with a pencil. Use a level and a yardstick to mark horizontal lines on the wall with a pencil. When measuring for the pattern repeat, always measure from your established marked lines, not from the last stenciled motif you completed, to avoid compounding any errors.

MARKING WALL BORDERS

To create a straight guideline for your border, first determine the height at which you want your stencil. Then use a tape measure to measure the distance from the floor or ceiling to the desired location on the wall and mark a dot. Place dots at this height at about 3' intervals. Place a pushpin on each dot and tie a string from pin to pin.

A few push pins and some string create taut guidelines without marring the wall.

PLANNING MOTIF COLORS

IN early examples of stenciling, we see heavily applied paint in harsh colors. The traditional stencils were somewhat naive, but the effect was charming and cheerful. This rather primitive style had and continues to have its place. However, with the availability of new paints, thoughtfully designed stencils, and subtly applied paint, stenciling can be a sophisticated, harmonious, and elegant addition to any home or office.

Just as I design the stencil motifs to echo the mood and furnishings of the room, I choose colors from the items in the room. For example, I might pick up the colors of the leaves and flowers in a chintz-covered sofa or the colors in a painting or quilt hanging on the wall. I prefer to use several shades of each color and vary them as I work around the room. Think of stenciled designs as accessories in the overall design of the room.

For smaller objects and furniture, look again at the surrounding elements of the room to help you decide the colors. For example, a table in a forties-style kitchen can repeat the colors in your favorite dishes or a cookie jar or the curtains.

The raspberry design in this print inspired the coordinating wall border.

Consider the mood you want to create. Do you want a north woods theme? Try forest greens, browns, or perhaps red-and-black check. Evoke a beach-cottage feeling with light blues, whites, and sandy yellows. For a garden room, stencil with greens, roses, blues, and yellows. Consider muted neutrals for a more sophisticated look.

I often choose a palette by studying an object that appeals to me, like a scarf or a plate. Remember to look not only at the colors but also at the amount of space that is covered by that color. This helps you decide on the proportions of each color.

WORKING WITH BACKGROUND COLORS

SINCE the luminous effect of beautiful stenciling depends on allowing the background color to show through the paint, the choice of a background color for the room is important to the overall outcome. Blue paint stenciled on a light yellow wall will take on a green cast. Of course, this is not a problem if this is the effect you want. Obviously, not every room can be painted white or off-white for the sake of the stenciling. To solve this problem, take a small amount of white or off-white stencil paint and mix in a drop of the wall color. Apply this as a light first coat of stencil paint. Allow this white paint to dry for about one minute: this becomes the primer. Then proceed to stencil the design in your chosen colors directly over the primer. This trick will allow you to achieve a soft translucent design in

the colors you want and eliminate show-through of the wall color.

Also, if you stencil colors on a dark surface such as stained wood, the paint tends to disappear on the dark background. To alleviate this problem, try applying the stencil paint in the colors you desire. Before you remove the stencil, add a light mist of white or off-white paint to the outer edges of the design. This will create a soft contrast to the dark wood while allowing you to use the colors you desire.

When stenciling over a dark background, add a fine mist of a light color to the outer edges of the design.

Always paint a few pieces of cardboard with your background color. Test your stencil colors on the cardboard to get a sense of what your design will look like. You can easily make any adjustments to your colors at this time. Testing on cardboard will also assist you in judging how much paint to apply.

APPLYING THE PAINT

A LIGHT application of paint is the key and cardinal rule for beautiful stenciling. For the stencil to be subtle and luminous, some of the background must show through the colored paint. Apply the paint using an up-and-down motion with the brush, called stippling or pouncing. This technique is used with a stiff-bristled brush or foam pouncing tool. You can also apply the paint with a sponge, using the same pouncing motion.

Start in the areas of the shape that are away from the light source or toward the base of the design. Gradually allow the paint to fade into lighter areas. The painting styles shown in this book depend on a light application of paint. Remember that as you apply the paint through the stencil, some of the paint will remain on the stencil itself. This makes judging the intensity of the color difficult. While holding most of the stencil in place, try peeling back just one corner to peek at the color underneath. Try to combine lighter and darker areas of paint in one motif. Remember that if you make a mistake or are disappointed in the painting, you can simply wash the paint off or repaint the area with the original background paint and try again.

For fine, detailed work, cut a separate stencil and use a separate small brush for each color. In complex, dense designs, such as the ribboned dresser on page 30, I cut one stencil for the ribbons and one for the flowers. However, for slightly larger work, simply cut one stencil and tape over any stencil windows where you want to avoid blending the colors.

Allowing some of the colors to overlap each other creates the lovely transparencies of watercolor painting.

Whenever possible, I prefer to use a single stencil to paint all the colors in a design. I like to allow (even encourage) the colors to drift into each other's color areas. When using a single stencil for several different colors, I often deliberately tap some paint into an adjacent stencil window. For example, I often let the green paint of the leaves drift onto the maroon of some raspberries and vice versa. This, after all, mimics the way our eyes perceive the colors of nature. The tonal shading varies and enlivens the stenciling.

Rather than mixing a color and applying it to the wall I prefer to allow the colors to mix during the stenciling process. This is another trick of the professional. Instead of buying or mixing an olive green, I prefer to paint the area with a light green and then repaint a thin mist of brown over the green to achieve the color I want. This method, first used by the Impressionists, creates a translucent and delicate effect.

APPLYING ACRYLIC PAINT

ACRYLIC paint specifically designed for craft projects comes in 2-oz. plastic bottles. When you paint with liquid paint it is essential to keep the brush almost dry and apply the paint in thin layers with a tapping or pouncing motion, building up the color in a soft cloud.

1. Pour a few drops of paint onto your palette. Tap the tip of your brush in the color.

2. Pounce the brush on a folded paper towel in an up-and-down motion until only a mist of paint is produced. See "Bottle and Jar Paints" page 7.

3. Starting on the outer edges of the stencil window, work the color in the appropriate area with a pouncing gesture. Try not to drag the brush from side to side; rather, use a strong tapping motion.

Pounce the paint over the stencil window.

APPLYING CRAYON PAINT

OIL-BASED stencil paints are usually sold in the form of thick crayons. However, the paint is still applied with a brush.

1. Rub the sealing coat off the crayon with a paper towel. Then rub some of the crayon color onto your palette (this can be a saucer, a paper plate, a disposable container, or just a free corner of your stencil). Work the color onto your brush.

2. Apply the color in the appropriate areas of the stencil. Using a dabbing or pouncing motion, build up the color gradually.

APPLYING SPRAY PAINT

STENCILING with spray paint is an excellent option for very large projects. Spray paint comes in hundreds of colors, dries instantly, and creates a lovely mist of color. However there are some disadvantages to using spray paint. The paint zooms out of the can at an astonishing speed, making it hard to control and creating a mist of paint that covers everything.

1. When stenciling with spray paint, mask the surrounding areas with coated freezer paper (available in the canning section of your supermarket). Cut the freezer paper in 6' strips and hold it in place with painter's masking tape. Use a succession of fine, light coats of spray paint to achieve subtle colors and the misty look that is so desirable in stenciling. Use a manila folder to aim and localize the spray and guide it toward a specific stencil window.

2. Spray the darker areas first and create a three-dimensional look by painting the base of a solid shape slightly darker. Darken the side of the object that is farther from the light source. Always allow some of the base coat to show through the stenciling.

If you are uncertain about spray paint, buy just one can and practice on cardboard. Try starting the spray and walking toward your "target." Try deflecting the spray with a manila folder. Practice until you feel confident enough to work on your project. This may take a can or two of paint but will pay rich dividends in satisfaction.

NOTE: *See "Safety Precautions" on page 8.*

CREATING SPECIAL EFFECTS

CONSIDER adding interest and individuality to your stenciling by experimenting with some simple techniques. Practice on cardboard or scrap paper and test for durability.

✦ Try stenciling a design over sponge painting.

Kokopeli figures are stenciled on a sponged wall.

✦ Add an interesting checked or plaid appearance to your stenciling by placing a layer of ½" chicken wire over the stencil window and painting through it. Try different sizes of wire fencing, or screening called hardware cloth.

Stenciling through wire screening gives the house on the right a checked appearance.

✦ For a softer, more pastel, accent, or to add shading lines, use colored pencils.

✦ Experiment with ink or felt-tip pens. Try adding accent lines, shading, and perhaps even some outlining.

I marked the sashing strips on this quilt with a permanent marking pen. I also outlined birds for more definition.

✦ Create depth in your designs by drawing pencil outlines on your design on the side away from the light source. Use a soft pencil (#B4 or #B6) obtainable at an art- or drafting-supply store. With your thumb, smudge the penciled lines to give depth and dimension to your work. I used this technique to produce the quilting lines on the quilt on page 5.

✦ Feel free to add some touches of your own to your stenciled designs. Try drawing embellishments such as dots or dashes or squiggles.

CLEANING UP

CLEANING BRUSHES

CLEAN brushes carefully after each use. Rinse off the damp paint and wash the brush in warm water and dishwashing liquid to remove all traces of paint. Dry the brush before using it again. For bristle brushes, wrap a short strip of masking tape around the bristles to keep them straight while they dry. If you have only one or two brushes and cannot wait for the brush to air dry, you can speed up the process with a hair dryer on the lowest setting. If you have been using an oil-based paint, thoroughly clean the brush with the appropriate solvent. Finish by washing with warm, soapy water.

CLEANING STENCILS

USE a soft cloth or paper towel to clean acetate stencils. Gently try to wash the paint away from the holes in the stencil. Bits of dust, paint, and adhesive collect around the edges of the holes and blur the edges. Careful cleaning will prolong the life of the stencil. A soft rag moistened with alcohol or mineral spirits (paint thinner) cleans excess adhesive from the stencil. Store your stencils flat and separated with sheets of freezer paper.

CLEANING PALETTES

PAINT dried on a paper palette can be thrown away. Allow the paint on a glass or plastic palette to dry completely. Then pour water on the palette and allow it to soak for about an hour. After soaking for about an hour the paint will peel away. By throwing the peeled paint in the trash rather than rinsing the wet paint down the drain you will help in a small way to protect our water from pollution.

Practice your stenciling techniques by making some greeting cards or gift bags. You can tie several cards together with a length of ribbon or raffia to make a gift set.

BEFORE TACKLING A big project, make some stenciled greeting cards or gift bags as a fun way to practice your stenciling skills. They are inexpensive to make. To make greeting cards, cut in half a piece of card-stock paper measuring 8½" x 11"; then fold each piece in half to make 2 cards measuring 4¼" x 5½". Envelopes for this size card are readily available in packets of twenty or twenty-five. Or purchase a set of blank greeting cards and envelopes at a stationery store. Blank gift bags are available at stationery or party supply stores.

INSTRUCTIONS

1. Choose any stencil design on pages 70–95 that fits to decorate your cards or gift bags. Follow the instructions for "Making Your Own Stencils" on pages 10–11.

2. Center the stencil over the front of a card or bag. Use removable tape to hold the card and stencil in place.

3. Pour a small puddle of paint onto your palette. Dip the tip of a brush in the paint; pounce excess paint off on a paper towel.

4. Stencil the design, following the instructions for "Applying the Paint" on pages 12–14. Use a different brush to stencil each color of paint.

5. Carefully peel off the tape and remove the stencil from the card or gift bag.

This section of the book is filled with inspiring project ideas. Each project or project grouping contains several coordinating stencils. Use the stencils provided to stencil on walls, furniture, fabrics, and accessories. You can use the stencils as they are, enlarging them or reducing them as necessary, or adapt them for a custom fit on your own furnishings. With the many projects offered here, you're sure to find lots of ideas for stenciling around your home.

PROJECTS

This little collection of furniture for a child's room was assembled from a thrift store, our bottomless basement, and an unfinished furniture store. An easy stenciled quilt and a chair-rail wall border of houses complement the furniture grouping. Instructions are given for the small chest, the quilt, and the wall border. The chest with the cherry knobs, the rocker, and the bed are projects made with adapted stencils from the collection.

INSTRUCTIONS
Stenciling

NOTE: *Refer to the general instructions for "Applying the Paint" on pages 12–14.*

1. Use the design on page 72 to make a stencil of the birds on twigs. Follow the instructions for "Making Your Own Stencils" on pages 10–11.

2. Apply a light coat of spray adhesive to the back of the stencil; allow to dry for about 5 minutes. Adhere to the front of the chest.

3. Pour a small puddle of each paint color, about the size of a quarter, onto your palette. Dip the tip of a brush in the green paint; pounce the excess paint off on a paper towel.

I DECIDED TO *paint the drawers of this chest with a base coat of cream and the sides and top with pine green. I also added a narrow band of coordinating green paint around the sides of the chest for accent. Before giving your chest a base coat, follow "Preparing Surfaces for Stenciling" on page 11.*

MATERIALS

+ Stencil design as listed below
+ Acetate or card-stock paper
+ Spray adhesive
+ Stencil paint in brown, red, blue, gold, and green
+ Palette
+ Brushes
+ Paper towels
+ Permanent black marker
+ Ruler
+ White colored pencil
+ Painter's masking tape
+ Latex paint in pine green (left over from base coat)
+ Acrylic paint in hunter green and mint

4. Pounce the brush over the leaf holes of the stencil. Start at the twig end of the leaf and continue out to the tip. Try adding a little more paint to the lower parts of the leaves to shade them and give them a little more depth.

5. Next, stencil the twigs and branches. Pounce a little of the leaf color onto the twigs and stems.

6. Experiment stenciling the birds on a scrap of cardboard and then stencil them on the chest. Although they are cut as single shapes, I like to paint them with several colors. Stencil the body blue, the breast red, and the beak gold.

7. Stencil the cherries with red paint. Continue stenciling over each window opening as shown below.

8. Peel the stencil from the chest.

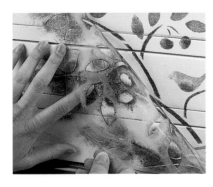

9. Draw eyes on each of the birds with a permanent black marker.

Contrasting Narrow Band

1. Using a ruler and the white pencil, draw a line 1½" in from the edges on each side of the chest.

2. Draw a second line ⅜" inside the first line.

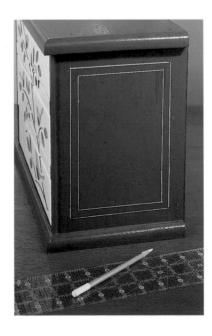

3. Place painter's masking tape along the outer pencil line. Place a second set of masking tape strips along the inner pencil line.

4. Paint the exposed ⅜" strip between the tape lines with a very thin coat of the pine green base paint. Leave the tape in place and let the paint dry. This will insure that you have a clean, crisp line of accent paint when you paint with the accent color.

5. Paint the strip between the tape lines again, this time with hunter green on the bottom and left-side bands and mint on the top and right-side bands; miter the corners where the two paint colors meet. When you are painting a light color over a dark one, you may have to paint a second coat of the accent colors.

6. Allow the paint to dry and gently remove the masking tape.

IF YOU PURCHASE pre-quilted fabric, all you have to do to make this quilt is finish the edges—and of course stencil the design, which is the fun part.

MATERIALS

+ Stencil designs as listed below
+ Acetate or card-stock paper
+ 1¼ yds. of 45"-wide pre-quilted, light-colored, cotton fabric
+ Scissors
+ Masking tape
+ Permanent marking pen
+ Stencil paint in cobalt, medium blue, antique blue, hunter green, blue-green, red, brown, and gold
+ Palette
+ Brushes
+ Paper towels
+ 1¼ yds. cotton backing fabric, if pre-quilted fabric does not have a cotton backing
+ ¾ yd. dark green fabric for the finishing strips
+ Iron and ironing board
+ Sewing machine and general sewing tools
+ Thread to match fabrics

INSTRUCTIONS

NOTE: *Refer to the general instructions for "Applying the Paint" on pages 12–14.*

1. Use the design on page 71 to make stencils of the quilt blocks. Follow the instructions for "Making Your Own Stencils" on pages 10–11.

2. Place the pre-quilted fabric on a clean tabletop and trim the edges to make it a true rectangle. Tape the fabric to the table to prevent it from shifting.

3. Draw grid lines down the length of the fabric with the permanent marking pen; start marking 1½" from one long raw edge. Space the first 2 lines 1¼" apart, then 6" apart. Continue in this manner, alternating 1¼" bands (sashing strips) and 6" bands. Draw 5 narrow bands and 4 wide ones. Then draw a line 1½" from one short edge. Continue to draw narrow and wide bands across the fabric from side to side in the same manner as before. Draw 6 narrow bands and 5 wide ones.

4. Using the lines as guides, stencil the quilt blocks onto the 6" squares marked on the fabric. Stencil the squares on the quilt where the sashing strips intersect. Stencil the birds in the center of each quilt block. Clean the stencil and use the reverse side to stencil some of the birds. Outline some of the stencil lines, if necessary, with the pen.

5. Trim the fabric a scant 1½" beyond the outer sashing strips.

6. If your quilted fabric does not have a cotton backing, cut a piece of cotton fabric the same size as the quilted fabric. Pin the quilted fabric and the cotton fabric wrong sides together. Stitch the 2 fabrics together ¼" from the edges.

7. Cut 2 finishing strips 4" x 34½" for the upper and lower edges of the quilt. Also cut 2 finishing strips 4" x 41½" for the sides of the quilt. Press up ¼" on both long edges of each strip.

8. Unfold one pressed edge on one short strip, and place right sides together 1¼" from the upper edge of the quilt front. Stitch on the fold line. Fold the strip to the back of the quilt, encasing the raw edges. Pin on the back, just covering the stitching line. Repeat on the lower edge. Stitch the finishing strips to the side edges in the same manner. Fold in ½" excess at the ends. Slipstitch the ends closed and slipstitch the strips to the back of the quilt.

THIS ROW OF *houses is a nice complement to this collection of children's furniture. Plan the border to finish with a complete motif at the corners of the room. Add an extra tree or bush if necessary to adjust the spacing.*

Plan the desired location of the wall stencil. If you choose to place it on the wall just under the ceiling, cut the stencil exactly parallel to the edge of the sheet of acetate. This enables you to hold the edge of the stencil against the ceiling to keep the border perfectly horizontal as you stencil. You may also choose to position the border at chair-rail height, as shown in the photo.

MATERIALS

+ Ruler
+ Pencil
+ Push pins
+ String
+ Stencil design as listed below
+ Acetate or card-stock paper
+ Palette
+ Paper towels
+ Brushes
+ Spray adhesive
+ Stencil paint in pine green, hunter green, mint green, brown, slate, olive, red, gold, and dark blue

INSTRUCTIONS

NOTE: *Refer to the general instructions on page 9 for "Design Suggestions" and the general instructions for "Applying the Paint" on pages 12–14.*

1. Follow the instructions for "Marking Wall Borders" on page 11.

2. Use the design on page 70 to make a stencil of the neighborhood wall border. Follow the instructions for "Making Your Own Stencils" on pages 10–11.

3. Lightly spray the back of your stencil with adhesive; allow to dry for about 5 minutes. When ready, place the stencil against the wall and press it lightly into position.

4. Stencil each color of the design on the wall. Move the stencil to the next section of wall and repeat as necessary. Use the photo as a guide to color placement.

CHEST WITH CHERRY KNOBS

This chest is *just right for holding the treasures of childhood. The drawer knobs on the chest are clusters of cherries placed in a pattern to alternate with the stenciled birds.*

ROCKER

The red rocker *looks both stately and cozy. Just a few clusters of birds and leaves maintain the structural beauty of the chair, while the "rocking bird" sitting atop a spring adds a touch of whimsy. Any toddler would love to sit on the lap of a grown-up in this simple red rocker.*

THE DECISION TO *give this old homemade youth bed a new life was an easy one. I gave it two coats of cream paint, then painted the trim pine green. To make a custom stencil for this bed, I taped a piece of acetate to a side panel of the bed, and traced an outline of the shape onto the acetate. Then I simply adapted the stencil design of birds on twigs (page 72) to fit the side panels. I used this same process to adapt the stencil for the head and foot of the bed. For the foot of the bed, I turned the stencil into a tree by adding a trunk. I also added a heart in the center of the branches and some patches of grass below. Stencil the bed in the same manner as for the small chest, following steps 2–8 on pages 20–21. Stencil each of the birds a solid color.*

CELEBRATING WOMEN IN THE ARTS

RIE MUÑOZ

The huge old chest has had many lives in our family and probably several more before it came to us. It held bathroom linens for about five years before it became a sewing chest. It served as a cat maternity ward and then, after a good scrubbing, became a friendly kitchen cupboard. A set of cobalt blue plates with stars and moons inspired its current decoration with paint.

I used cobalt blue paint on the chest and rocker. When you are looking at paint chips, look for blues close to the lavender and purple section rather than those close to the turquoises. Before painting your base coat, follow "Preparing Surfaces for Stenciling" on page 11.

After stenciling my design and waiting several days for the paint to cure, I sealed the furniture with a coat of satin-finish polyurethane. Complete instructions are given for stenciling the chest. I made the coordinating rocker using the same techniques.

MATERIALS

+ Cobalt blue latex paint (left over from the base coat)
+ Disposable container
+ White latex paint
+ Rubber gloves
+ Sea sponge
+ Cardboard
+ Paper towels
+ Stencil designs as listed below
+ Acetate or card-stock paper
+ Stencil paint in white, pale yellow, and dark yellow
+ Palette
+ 1" stencil brush
+ Spray adhesive
+ Satin-finish polyurethane

INSTRUCTIONS

NOTE: *Refer to the general instructions for "Applying the Paint" on pages 12–14.*

1. Pour about ½ cup of the cobalt base paint into a disposable container. Add about a tablespoon of white paint and mix thoroughly. Check the color. It should be lighter than the cobalt and slightly chalky. If it is not light enough, add more white and mix it thoroughly until you have a color lighter than the cobalt but still fairly close to it.

2. Wearing rubber gloves, dip a sea sponge into the paint and squeeze it out thoroughly. Tap the sponge on a piece of cardboard to make sure only a small amount of paint will be transferred to the chest. Also, wipe off your rubber glove occasionally with a paper towel to prevent paint buildup. When you have practiced with the sponge a little, lightly sponge the entire chest.

3. Use the sun, moon, and star designs on pages 73–74 to make stencils. Follow the instructions for "Making Your Own Stencils" on pages 10–11.

4. Stencil faint stars on the chest in a variety of sizes using the chalky blue paint and the sea sponge. With your left hand, hold the desired star stencil on the chest. With your right hand, sponge the star. Repeat over the entire chest, spacing the stars evenly. Stand back every so often and check to see that you have fairly even coverage. You can always add more sponge paint or stars later.

5. Using the pale yellow paint and a 1" stencil brush, stencil stars in random clusters on the chest, leaving them out of the area where the large sunburst will be stenciled.

6. Using the dark yellow paint, stencil some more stars within your random clusters. Also stencil a large moon in some clusters.

7. Spray a light mist of adhesive on the back of the stencils of the sun face and sun rays; allow to dry for about 5 minutes. Place the stencils on the chest, centering the face inside the rays.

8. Stencil the face of the sun with light yellow paint. Stencil the stars and small moon on the face with light yellow paint. Remove the circle from the center of the sun. Pounce lightly around the edge of the circle, inside the rays, with light yellow paint. Use less and less paint as you pounce toward the inside of the circle.

9. Place the crescent stencil on the upper-right side of the center circle of the sun, and using a light touch, paint the edges of the crescent with light yellow paint. Remove the stencil.

10. Using dark yellow paint, stencil the rays of the sun up to ¼" from the inside circle, covering the cobalt paint completely.

11. Wait several days and then seal with polyurethane.

ROCKER

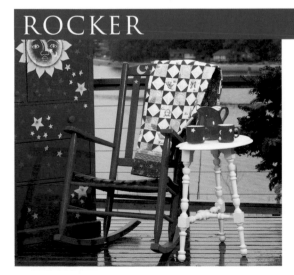

I painted this rocker with cobalt blue paint to match the chest, then sponged it lightly as described in steps 1 and 2 on page 28. I selected the smaller stars and cresent moon designs and stenciled the back of the rocker randomly.

RIBBONS & FLOWER

The dresser was my inspiration for this romantic collection of stencil projects. Its unabashed femininity cried out for ribbons and flowers. The large lower drawer provided ample space to feature some elaborate stenciling. The little bouquets on the upper drawers are repeated on the top surface and inside the drawers. More ribbons and flowers are painted on the apron, and ribbons are stenciled around the mirror. Since every piece of furniture has different dimensions, I have included a smaller version of the ribbon-and-flower swag in the book as well. Use the reducing and enlarging features of a copy machine to change the size of the design to fit your own project. Notice that the ribbons are printed as individual sections that you can trace to fit your own mirror or lampshade. Complete instructions are given for the dresser and the lampshade. The wall border, mirror, and chair are easy adaptations. Before starting these projects, refer to "Preparing Surfaces for Stenciling" on page 11.

DRESSER

I FOUND THIS *dainty little dress-er at a thrift store. Its price was not really all that thrifty, but its oval mirror, scalloped apron, and feminine aura called to me. It had been very badly abused, so I decid-ed to give it a good scrub. After cleaning it, I sanded it lightly and coated it with a high-quality primer and two coats of a pale pink latex paint. Once all the sten-ciling was complete I coated it with an antiquing glaze to give it a gentle old patina.*

The paint departments of large home-improvement centers sell a variety of glazes for this purpose. I purchased the store brand of a simple antiquing glaze and applied it with a soft brush. Use long, smooth strokes and follow the direction of the grain of the wood. Make long, even strokes until you have the effect you desire. Let the glaze dry overnight and then apply a second or even third coat for a darker finish.

MATERIALS

- Tape measure
- Stencil designs as listed below
- Acetate or card-stock paper
- Spray adhesive
- Stencil paint in blue, yellow, pink, raspberry, and green
- Palette
- Brushes
- Paper towels

INSTRUCTIONS

NOTE: *Refer to the general instructions for "Applying the Paint" on pages 12–14.*

1. Measure your furniture and plan your stencil design to fit the drawer front and apron. Use the flower clusters and ribbon-and-flower swags on pages 75–76 to make stencils. Follow the instruc-tions for "Making Your Own Stencils" on pages 10–11. Make a separate stencil for the ribbon and the flower elements of the large and small swags.

2. Lightly spray the back of the stencil of the ribbon portion of the large ribbon-and-flower swag with adhesive. Allow the adhesive to dry for about 5 min-utes. When ready, place the stencil against the large drawer and press it lightly into position.

3. Stencil the ribbon with blue paint. For shading, stencil more heavily on the narrow portions of the ribbon. Allow to dry. Repeat step 2 for the flower portion of the design. Using a different brush for each color, stencil each color in the flower stencil. Stencil some areas of the flowers more heavily to indicate shaded areas. Gently remove the stencil from the dresser.

4. Repeat the stenciling process for the apron of the dresser using the small ribbon-and-flower swag. Also stencil flower clusters on the center of the top drawer fronts and on dresser top as desired.

MIRROR

FOLLOW STEPS 1–3 *on page 33 for the lampshade to make a custom sten-cil to fit around a mirror frame. Stencil the ribbon garland along the top and bottom of the frame. (Follow step 4 on page 33. Ignore the reference to the flower cluster.)*

WALL BORDER

FOLLOW STEPS 1–4 *for the wall border on page 23. Substitute the ribbon-and-flower wall border design in step 2. Use the photo on pages 30–31 as a guide to color placement. Stencil more heavily along the nar-rowest portions of the ribbon for shading.*

LAMPSHADE

STENCILING IS AN *easy way to dress up a ready-made lampshade. You can stencil any smooth fabric or paper shade.*

MATERIALS

+ Freezer paper
+ Stencil designs as listed below
+ Access to a photocopy machine
+ Acetate or card-stock paper
+ Spray adhesive
+ Stencil paint in blue, yellow, pink, and green
+ Palette
+ Brushes
+ Paper towels

INSTRUCTIONS

NOTE: *Refer to the general instructions for "Applying the Paint" on pages 12–14.*

1. Cut a piece of freezer paper and gently wrap the paper around the lampshade; fold the paper along the lower edges to crease. Overlap sheets of paper and tape together as necessary.

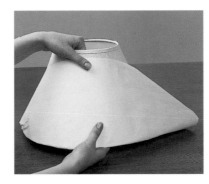

2. Using the creases as a placement guide, trace the ribbon garland (page 76) onto the freezer paper. Rotate the stencil design as necessary to keep the design aligned evenly with the crease in the paper.

3. Transfer the design from the freezer paper to a piece of acetate and make a stencil. Follow the instructions for "Making Your Own Stencils" on pages 10–11. If desired, make a stencil of a flower cluster (page 75).

4. Lightly spray the back of the stencil with adhesive; allow to dry 5 minutes. Press the stencil onto the lampshade. Stencil the ribbon with blue paint, stenciling more heavily over the narrowest portions of the ribbon. Add a flower cluster above the bow at the center front of the shade as shown in the photo (left). Gently remove the stencil from the shade.

TIP

To protect the shape of the shade while you are stenciling the designs, lay a thick magazine over your knee and then place the shade over the magazine with your knee positioned inside the shade.

CHAIR

FOR THIS COORDINATING *chair I used the same small ribbon-and-flower swag (page 76) as for the apron on the back of the dresser. To stencil the chair back, use the instructions for the dresser on page 32 as a guide.*

RASPBERRIES COLLE

This grouping consists of a desk, window cornice, wall border, and chair. The wall stencil and the cornice are arranged to form a continuous border around the room. Specific instructions are given for the desk and the cornice. Use stencils from the collection to make a coordinating wall border and chair.

THE ADVENT OF *foam board has greatly simplified the process of making beautiful cornices. Foam board consists of a sheet of fine-grained substance similar to Styrofoam between two pieces of strong, white paper. The boards are very lightweight and easy to cut and are useful for creating rigid shapes that do not require strength.*

Think of a cornice as a box with two sides missing. Start with a large piece of foam board cut to the width of the window, including the window frame, plus the distance the cornice must extend from the wall on each side (the return). If you need to piece foam board together for a wide cornice, butt two pieces together and cover the seam with duct tape. The cornice shown stands 5" from the wall, so I cut the length of the foam board to the length of the window, 70", plus 10" for the returns for a total of 80".

Traditionally, cornices are made about 10" to 15" high. The one shown measures 10" high, so I cut the width of the foam core 10", plus 5" for the return across the top for a total of 15". To put it simply, I cut the foam board to measure 80" x 15". Follow the directions on page 37 to make a foam-board cornice covered with lightweight quilt batting and fabric. Stencil the border design across the cornice; then stencil the wall border as on page 39 so the pattern of the raspberries continues.

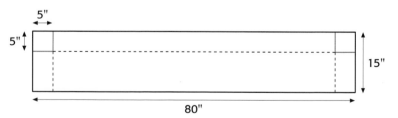

Cut on solid lines. Score on dashed lines.

Fold on dashed lines to create the box shape.

MATERIALS

+ Foam board
+ Craft knife
+ Pencil
+ Duct tape
+ Quilt batting
+ Tacky glue
+ Straight pins
+ Fabric for cornice
+ Stencil designs as listed below
+ Acetate or card-stock paper
+ Spray adhesive
+ Stencil paint in green, raspberry, brown, and gold
+ Palette
+ Paper towels
+ Brushes
+ Two 5" long nails

INSTRUCTIONS

NOTE: *Refer to the general instructions for "Applying the Paint" on pages 12–14.*

1. Cut the foam board to fit your window as described on page 36. Lay the board on a flat surface and mark the measurements on the board.

2. Draw a line the length of the board, 5" (the return measurement) from one long edge of the board. Draw a line at each short end of the board, 5" (the return measurement) from the edges.

3. Score the board on all marked lines with a craft knife. To score the board, cut through the first layer of heavy paper, but do not cut all the way through the board. Cut away the 5" squares that have been scored in the two corners of the board as shown on page 36.

4. Gently fold along the scored lines and tape the edges together at the corners with duct tape. If you pieced foam board together for additional length, cut a small piece of foam board to place over each seam on the back side for reinforcement. Secure the reinforcement pieces with duct tape.

5. Cut a piece of lightweight quilt batting 3" larger than the original board dimensions on all sides. Cover the board with the batting, wrapping excess batting to the back around the edges; cut away excess batting at the top corners. Secure batting in place with tacky glue and straight pins.

6. Cut your cornice fabric 4" larger than the original board dimensions on all sides. Cover the cornice with fabric, wrapping the excess around the edges to the back. Make a diagonal fold at the upper corners on the sides to fold out the excess fabric. Secure the fabric in place with straight pins and tacky glue. Insert the pins into the foam board at an angle.

7. Use the designs on page 77 to make stencils of the wall and cornice border and the three birds. Follow the instructions for "Making Your Own Stencils" on pages 10–11.

8. Lightly spray the back of your border stencil with adhesive. Allow to dry for about 5 minutes. When ready, place the stencil on the cornice and press it lightly into position. I placed my stencil 1" up from the lower long edge of the cornice.

9. While supporting the cornice on a table, start stenciling on the left side and continue working toward the right. Stencil each color of the design on the cornice fabric, using a different brush for each paint color. Pounce a small amount of brown paint around the stem ends of the leaves and along some leaf edges. Gently remove the stencil and reposition it on the next section of cornice fabric and repeat. At the end of the cornice, mark that place on the stencil as the spot to start stenciling on the wall.

10. Stencil the three birds randomly along the raspberry cornice.

11. To attach the cornice to the wall, pound a 5" nail at each end of the window the desired distance above the window frame. Only an inch of the nail should be in the wall with 4" sticking out. Simply rest the cornice on the 2 nails.

THIS LITTLE DESK, *a grimy, greenish yellow, sat unwanted in the corner of a neighborhood secondhand store. A little primer and a coat of light green latex paint revealed its lovely shape and readied it for a bit of stenciling.*

MATERIALS

+ Ruler
+ Pencil
+ Painter's masking tape
+ Brushes
+ Latex paint in light green to match the chest and in medium green
+ Stencil designs as listed below
+ Acetate or card-stock paper
+ Permanent pen
+ Stencil paint in green, raspberry, brown, and gold

INSTRUCTIONS

NOTE: *Refer to the general instructions for "Applying the Paint" on pages 12–14.*

1. Use a ruler to draw a faint pencil line 2" in from the outer edge of the desk.

2. Place a strip of painter's masking tape on the top of the desk inside the marked line. Lightly paint the border. First paint a light coat of the light green paint; be sure the paint spreads over the line where the tape meets the border. This will insure that you have a perfectly clean, crisp line on the outer border. When the light green paint is dry, paint the outer borders of the desk with medium green paint. On this piece of furniture I also painted the back apron, the front and side edges, the drawer edges, and parts of the legs with medium green paint.

3. Use the raspberry designs on pages 77 and 85 to make stencils of the raspberry clusters and the border. Follow the instructions for "Making Your Own Stencils" on pages 10–11. With your permanent pen, draw a thin, straight line through the middle of the border stencil.

4. Place the stencil with the line right on the place where the medium green border meets the light green on the desk.

5. Stencil the border on one side of the desk with green paint using one side of the stencil. Move the stencil and continue the border until you reach the corner. Slide the stencil a bit to fit the little motif over the corner. Paint the corner motif and then continue stenciling the border around the top of the desk. Stencil a border on the front drawer and sides of the desk in the same manner, positioning the border as desired.

6. Stencil raspberry clusters on the center of the lower front drawers and on the top front corners, top center back, and sides of the desk as desired.

WALL BORDER

MEASURE EACH WALL *and plan the positions of the repeat so that the motifs are not broken at the corners of the room. Adjust the spacing, if necessary, or make a little filler stencil to reach the corners. Follow steps 1–3 for the wall border on page 23. Substitute the design for the wall and cornice border on page 77 in step 2. Use the photo at left as a guide to color placement. Stencil the wall border as described in steps 9 and 10 of the cornice instructions on page 37.*

CHAIR

STENCIL A BORDER *on the bottom of the chair back using the border design on page 77. To make a bird stencil similar to the one shown on the top of the chair back, use the bluebird and flower on page 78. Substitute some raspberries from the raspberry cluster on page 77 for some of the leaves to coordinate this design with the remaining furnishings in the Raspberries collection.*

The little table served several years as a child's play table before it became a plant table on our porch. While on the porch, together with two Hitchcock chairs, it became the victim of a prolonged wind- and rainstorm. A bit of glue and some paint prepared the pieces for the stencil brush. To complement the ensemble, I also stenciled a china cabinet and a coordinating chair rail border. Complete instructions are given for the table and the china cabinet. The chairs and wall border are adaptations made with stencils from this collection.

TABLE

MATERIALS

+ Stencil designs as listed below
+ Acetate or card-stock paper
+ ⅛" and ¼" diameter round-hole paper-punch tools
+ Stencil paint in cobalt blue, navy, white, and light gray
+ Palette
+ Brushes
+ Paper towels
+ Spray adhesive
+ #6B pencil
+ Water-based polyurethane

INSTRUCTIONS

NOTE: *Refer to the general instructions for "Applying the Paint" on pages 12–14.*

1. Use the designs on pages 77, 78, 81, 83, 84, and 85 to make stencils of the lace tablecloth, the scalloped border, the twisted ribbon, the plate, the large bluebird, the raspberry clusters, and the cherries. Follow the instructions for "Making Your Own Stencils"

I WANTED A *very small and informal, random floral tablecloth pattern on the top of the table. However, cutting many tiny dainty flowers is very hard. So, I purchased two paper punches, one ¼" and one ⅛" with "long reach" handles. The punches both reached 3", so I cut a piece of stencil plastic 6" x 11" and punched ⅛" and ¼" round holes randomly all over the plastic. I then used my craft knife and extended some of the smaller circles into little leaves and quickly made a stencil with a tiny, lacy, random floral pattern. To prepare the table for stenciling, I applied a coat of light blue latex paint. Then I painted some accent rings on the turned areas on the table legs with contrasting blue acrylic paint.*

CHAIRS

PAINT THE CHAIRS *with light blue paint and paint any accent details with medium blue paint. I painted recessed areas on the large back spindles, the legs, and the chair seats with the accent color. Stencil a border (page 79) 2" from the edge of the seat. Stencil the bluebird-and-flower design (page 78) on the chair backs.*

on pages 10–11. Using paper-punch tools, follow the instructions on page 42 for cutting the designs in the lace tablecloth.

2. Stencil the table apron as desired using the border stencil and cobalt paint.

3. Use the stencil of the scalloped border to create the outer border of the tablecloth with white paint; place the scalloped edge of the stencil about 1" from the edge of the table. Stencil an inner border using the twisted ribbon and white paint; position the stencil ¼" inside the inner edge of the scalloped border.

4. Lightly apply spray adhesive to the wrong side of the stencil of the lace tablecloth; allow to dry for about 5 minutes. Stencil the center of the tablecloth with the lace-tablecloth stencil and white paint. Lift and move the stencil as necessary until the entire interior of the tablecloth is stenciled.

5. Stencil a plate at the center of each side of the table using the plate stencil and cobalt paint. Position the stencil ½" from the outer edge of the table. Pounce the area inside the plate outlines with white paint.

6. Stencil a bird, raspberry, or cherry cluster on the center of each plate with cobalt and navy paint.

7. Pounce shadows around the outer edges of each plate with light gray paint. Define the edges of the plates with a #6B pencil.

8. Apply several coats of water-based polyurethane to the table-top following the manufacturer's instructions.

TIP

Use a very cool, almost lavender, periwinkle blue on these "trompe l'oeil" dishes. The more pure ultramarine blues take on a turquoise cast when stenciled. If you are in doubt about the shade of blue to use, try dabbing a bit of paint directly onto a blue-and-white plate for comparison.

WALL BORDER

AN ATTRACTIVE PIECE *of molding from the local lumber store mimics a plate rail, and a stenciled collection of Limoges or Spode china adds a touch of humorous grandeur to this cheerful kitchen—a magnificent set of china and a good laugh, all for the price of a few bottles of paint. Choose a height above eye level for the plate rail. Then paint or stain the molding and nail it to the wall. Quickly stencil the china shapes (pages 78–85) onto sheets of scrap paper. (See "Making Your Own Stencils" on pages 10–11 and "Applying the Paint" on pages 12–14.) Use these to "arrange" the various pieces by tacking them above the plate rail. When you are happy with the arrangement, stencil them onto the wall. Deepen the shade of the color on the outer and lower edges of the china. Vary the sizes of the dishes used across the length of the wall. If you make a mistake, just paint it out with the wall color and try again.*

MATERIALS

+ Freezer paper
+ 30" x 48" light gray mat board for the cupboard doors
+ Utility knife
+ Pencil
+ Stencil designs as listed below
+ Acetate or card-stock paper
+ ⅛"- and ¼"-diameter round-hole paper-punch tools
+ Stencil paint in light gray, cobalt blue
+ Palette
+ Brushes
+ Paper towels
+ Satin-finish polyurethane
+ Sticky putty

INSTRUCTIONS

NOTE: *Refer to the general instructions for "Applying the Paint" on pages 12–14.*

1. Place a piece of freezer paper over the curved edge of the door. With your fingers, press the paper into the curve and create a crease in the shape of the curve. Trace the curved pattern onto your mat board and cut out the pieces using a utility knife. Lay the boards on a large table to stencil them.

2. Divide each piece of mat board into 3 sections. Draw a dark pencil line to create 2 matching shelves on each mat.

3. Use the design on page 84 to make the stencil of eyelet shelf edging. Follow the instructions for "Making Your Own Stencils" on pages 10–11. Draw grid lines on your stencil, with the cross marks of the grid lines right over

THE CHINA CABINET *looks like an impressive and complicated project, but it is really quite simple. The dishes are all easy to stencil. The complex look is achieved by creating the illusion that the dishes overlap. I painted the old china cabinet a clean, fresh white, then outlined the window openings and recessed areas of the cabinet doors with light blue. The glass had long been broken, so rather than replace the glass, I decided to paint a dream collection of antique blue-and-white Spode china on mat boards used for picture framing and use these as the door fronts.*

the points where holes will be punched. Use paper-punch tools to punch out the marked holes to create the eyelet effect. (For more information on cutting with paper punches, see the tip below.)

4. Align the straight edge of the eyelet shelf edging with the marked shelf lines. Stencil over the punched holes with light gray paint. Also stencil above and below the edges of the stencil with light gray paint to create the outline for the lace edging.

TIP

Paper punches are ideal for cutting the little holes of eyelet. The tricky part is learning to aim the punch for the right spot. I suggest placing a piece of tape with one edge right over the center of your punch hole. Use a permanent pen to draw a black line on the paper punch. Now do the same to mark the center of the hole from front to back. Remove the tape. Now all you have to do is line up the cross marks on your paper punch with the cross marks on the stencil.

5. Use the designs from the Blue Dish collection on pages 78–85 and make the dish stencils. Follow the instructions for "Making Your Own Stencils" on pages 10–11. Stencil the dishes in any arrangement you like. Mask off portions of dishes if other dishes will overlap them. See the tip on masking at right.

Plates. Stencil the plate design with cobalt blue. Omit the small flowers around the rim on some plates. Enhance the scalloped look on the plate rims by pouncing lines between the inner and outer rim lines. Stencil bluebird and raspberry clusters or other motifs from the collection on the centers of the plates. Pounce lightly inside the rim with light gray paint to shade.

Teapots and Pitchers. Pounce along the outer edges of the stencil to create the outline; leave a large white area in the center of the dish. Stencil a motif over the white center area to accent the piece. Use the interior stencil for teapot deisgn 2 and stencil along the edges of the wave design to outline.

Casserole Dish. Pounce lightly around the edges of the outline stencil to give the piece its shape; then place the interior stencil over the top and stencil the design lines heavily with cobalt.

Cups. Pounce along the edges of the stencil to create the outlines. For cup designs 1 and 3, leave a large white area in the center of the cups; then stencil a motif over the white area to accent the pieces. For cup design 4, stencil 2 vertical shadow lines in the center of the cup, connecting the scallop design at the top of the cup with the scallop design at the bottom of the cup.

6. Pounce light gray shadows around the china and on the shelves. Pick a direction for an imaginary light source. Pounce shadows on the opposite side of the light source around the china and shelf edging. Use the photo on page 44 as a guide.

7. Lightly coat the completed doors with polyurethane to protect them. Use sticky putty to hold the stenciled boards in place on the doors.

8. Stencil the twisted ribbon around each door. Stencil a bluebird motif on the center of each of the 3 bottom doors.

TIP

To make dishes look as though one piece is in front of the other, create a mask to cover the piece in front before stenciling the piece behind. A mask is a piece of paper that is cut exactly to match the outer edges of the stencil.

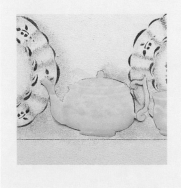

COLLECTION

As often happens, the legs of this table were in good condition but the tabletop was badly battered. I scrubbed the tabletop with kitchen cleanser, sanded it lightly, and stained it with a warm fruitwood color to match the legs. I rubbed the same stain lightly over the legs of the table to cover the scratches and dings. Next I decided to transform a group of dark, dignified Mediterranean modern chairs into cheerful seating with butter yellow paint and oak leaves and more acorns. When you work on stained wood or wood painted a medium color, the value of the wood contrasts only slightly with the colors of the designs. Painting with either a very dark or a very light color helps solve this problem. Think about the look you want—bright vibrant leaves or delicate subtle ones. I decided on subtlety for the table and vibrancy for the chairs—so much for logic. To complete the look throughout the room, I stenciled matching table linens, a hutch, and a chair-rail wall border. Complete instructions are given for the table. The linens, hutch, wall border, and chairs are all easy adaptations.

MATERIALS

+ Tape measure
+ Stencil designs as listed below
+ Access to photocopy machine
+ Acetate or card-stock paper
+ Spray adhesive
+ Stencil paint in taupe, raspberry, sage, brown, gold, tan, and rust
+ Palette
+ Brushes
+ Paper towels

INSTRUCTIONS

NOTE: *Refer to the general instructions for "Applying the Paint" on pages 12–14.*

1. Measure your tabletop. Plan for the long oak-leaf garland on page 87 to fit on a little less than half of the outer edge of the drop leaf. Make stencils of the long and short oak-leaf garlands. Follow the instructions for "Making Your Own Stencils" on pages 10–11.

2. Lightly spray the stencil of the long oak-leaf garland with adhesive and allow to set for 5 minutes. Place it on the left side of 1 drop leaf.

3. Stencil the left half of 1 drop leaf and then the left half of the other drop leaf. Stencil the twigs with taupe paint. Stencil some of the leaves and acorns with 2 or 3 colors of paint, stenciling some areas more heavily for a shaded effect.

4. Clean the stencil and reverse it from front to back to make a mirror image for the right half of the drop leaves. Stencil the design on the remaining halves of the drop leaves as before.

5. Stencil the side edges of the tabletop with the short oak-leaf garland, stenciling on each side of the drop leaves and in the center of each side between the drop leaves.

TABLE LINENS

STENCILING ON FABRIC *is as simple as stenciling on any other surface and gives a custom look to inexpensive table linens.*

Wash, dry, and press the place mats and napkins. Then stencil the place mats as you stenciled the table; use the photo as a guide for placement of the stencil designs. For the napkins stencil two leaves in the corner and accent with two acorns.

WALL BORDER & CHAIR

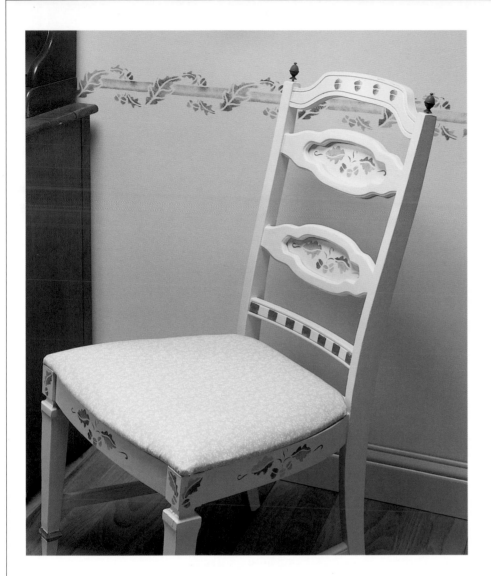

FOLLOW STEPS 1–4 *for the wall border, on page 23. Substitute the oak-leaf-border design on page 86 in step 2. Use the photo at left as a guide to color placement.*

For the chair, use the oak-leaf swag on page 86 to make a stencil. Stencil the swag design to the back of the chair and to the apron on the seat front and sides. Stencil an additional leaf and acorn over the top of each leg, just under the seat. Stencil acorns across the top of the chair back and stencil the checkered border on the bottom of the chair back. You can use the square in the quilt-blocks design on page 71 to make a square stencil for the checkered border. Acorn drawer pulls were painted and attached to the back of the chair for accent.

HUTCH

USE THE FLOWER *border on page 86 to make a stencil for this hutch. Stencil the design in a vertical stripe pattern, spacing the stripes evenly.*

K okopeli is a mythical, magical, musical trickster in the lore of the Southwest. His secretive reputation makes him the perfect decorative element in a subtle artistic scheme. By lightly painting his image on the walls along with some random triangles, you can create texture and interest in a room without dominating the space. To carry the Southwest theme into the furnishings, I stenciled an old chest with a center cross motif and repeated the triangle motifs from the walls on the sides. Instructions are given for the wall design and chest.

A SOFT SPONGING *of tan over a cream basecoat gives these walls a strong texture and readies them for the fun of the mythical Kokopeli figures. You can space the figures evenly for an allover effect, or if you prefer, march them around the room in single file to create a border. The project directions given below are for an allover look.*

MATERIALS

+ Stencil designs as listed below
+ Acetate or card-stock paper
+ Paper that matches the wall color
+ Removable tape
+ Spray adhesive
+ Stencil paint in pale umber
+ Palette
+ Brushes
+ Paper towels

INSTRUCTIONS

NOTE: *Refer to the general instructions for "Applying the Paint" on pages 12–14*

1. Use the designs on pages 88–90 to make the Kokopeli and triangles stencils. Follow the instructions for "Making Your Own Stencils" on pages 10–11.

2. Find the visual center of the wall. (See "Centering" on page 11.) Quickly stencil several figures on sheets of paper similar in color to the wall.

3. Using removable tape, tape the first figure slightly above and to the left of your designated center of the wall. Tape the remaining figures at 18" to 24" intervals. If possible, stand back to see how you like them. Adjust the spacing if necessary for a random, carefree look.

4. After working out the spacing of the figures, lightly spray the back of the stencils with adhesive; allow to dry for about 5 minutes. Stencil the figures on the wall at the designated locations. Consider tilting them slightly for a more lighthearted look.

5. Stencil portions of the triangles stencil between the Kokopeli figures as shown in the photo on pages 50–51. Tape off unwanted parts of the stencil as necessary.

My NEIGHBOR HAD *a lovely old teak chest with a deep scratch on the front, a definite gouge on the side, and one drawer knob missing. My friend and I exchanged a modest amount of money and the chest moved from her garage to mine. Then, of course, I immediately went out and spent almost double the price of the chest on new drawer pulls. By placing the stenciling over the damaged portions of the chest, I was able to hide the injuries and retain the beauty of the teak. Using black paint for the stenciling gave the chest a masculine look, and the added dabs of turquoise gave it just the right patina.*

MATERIALS

+ Stencil designs as listed below
+ Acetate or card-stock paper
+ Access to photocopy machine
+ Spray adhesive
+ Stencil paint in black and turquoise
+ Palette
+ Brushes
+ Paper towels

INSTRUCTIONS

NOTE: *Refer to the general instructions for "Applying the Paint" on pages 12–14.*

1. Use the designs on pages 88 and 90 to make stencils of the Southwest cross and triangles. Follow the instructions for "Making Your Own Stencils" on pages 10–11.

2. Determine the placement of the cross design on the center front of the chest. Mark the position of your stencil, centering the design from side to side.

3. Lightly spray the back of your Southwest cross stencil with adhesive; allow to dry for about 5 minutes. When ready, place the stencil against the drawers and press it lightly into position. Paint the first half of the design with black paint. Allow the paint to dry and, without pouncing your brush dry, dab on a bit of turquoise paint here and there.

4. Move the stencil and finish the second half of the design with black and then turquoise paint.

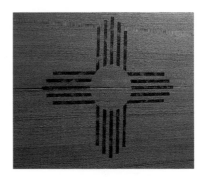

5. Lightly spray the back of the triangles stencil with adhesive. Position the triangles stencil lightly on the upper-left side of the chest so that both arms of the triangles are the same distance from and parallel to the edges of the chest.

6. Stencil the design with black paint. Allow the paint to dry and, without pouncing your brush dry, dab on a bit of turquoise paint here and there.

7. Move the stencil to the lower-right corner and stencil the design with black and then turquoise paint.

OLLECTION

The ivy swags lend a touch of romance to this collection. I used them around the room as a wall border, alternating bird nests with birds and bird nests with eggs in the center of the swags. The center drop leaf of the desk features a single swag bordered with a ribbon design. Complete instructions are given for the desk. The wall border, bed, night stand, and chair are easy variations (see page 57 for brief instructions for the wall border; see photos on these two pages and designs on page 91 to stencil the bed, night stand, and chair).

I BOUGHT THIS *desk at the Salvation Army for $7.95 in 1965. The sickly green paint that covered it hid whatever wood was underneath. I painted the desk gray blue and it has passed from the living room to the kitchen to the den and on through the rooms of our children. This year we rescued it from our basement where moisture had swollen the drawers and mildewed the legs. Some tender loving care and a quart of light cream latex paint brought it back to a respectable condition and readied the desk for a new life.*

MATERIALS

+ Ruler
+ Pencil
+ Painter's masking tape
+ Latex paint in light cream to match the chest and in tan
+ Brushes
+ Stencil designs as listed below
+ Acetate or card-stock paper
+ Permanent marking pen
+ Spray adhesive
+ Palette
+ Paper towels
+ Stencil paint in blue, sage, medium brown, dark brown, and red

INSTRUCTIONS

NOTE: *Refer to the general instructions for "Applying the Paint" on pages 12–14.*

1. Use a ruler and pencil to draw a faint pencil line 2" from the edge around the top and sides of the desk. Also draw a faint pencil line 2" from the edges of the drop leaf of the desk and around the 2 bottom drawers combined.

2. Place painter's masking tape 2" from the edge of the desktop just inside the marked lines. Lightly paint the 2" border in the light cream color. Be sure the cream paint spreads over the line where the tape meets the border. This will insure that you have a perfectly clean, crisp line on the border. When the light cream paint is dry, paint the outer borders of the desk with tan paint. Repeat for the sides, the leaf, and the bottom drawers. I also painted the top drawer, lower front of the desk, the apron, and part of the legs with tan paint.

3. Use the designs on pages 78 and 91 to make stencils (see pages 10–11) of the twisted ribbon, the ivy swag, the birds in nest, the bird nest and eggs, and the bird and chick.

4. With your permanent pen, draw a thin, straight line through the middle of the twisted ribbon. Lightly spray the back of your stencil with adhesive; allow to dry for about 5 minutes. Place the stencil on the desk with the marked line right on the place where the tan border meets the light cream.

5. Stencil the twisted ribbon around the top edges of the desk.

6. Reposition the stencil as necessary and continue across the

border until you reach the corner. If necessary, slide the stencil a bit to fit the little motif over the corner. Paint the corner motif and then continue stenciling the adjacent side. Continue in the same manner around the top of the desk. Repeat around the sides, the folding desk leaf, and the lower drawers.

7. Lightly spray the back of your ivy-swag stencil with adhesive; allow to dry for about 5 minutes. When ready, place the stencil over the drop leaf, centered from side to side.

8. Stencil the ivy swag on the drop leaf of the desk. The space available on the desk leaf was smaller than the design, so I adjusted the design by eliminating a few of the leaves and moving some of the leaves and berries. Start by stenciling the leaves sage; then tap a slight mist of brown or blue onto some of the leaves.

9. Stencil the rod brown and the ribbon and flowers blue. Stencil the berries red. Use medium brown and dark brown on the nest; pounce some brown paint onto the lower parts of the birds. Stencil the birds blue; make the outer edges of the birds a little darker than the centers to give them a chubby appearance.

10. Stencil the bird nest with eggs on one side of the desk and the bird and chick on the other. Position the ivy-swag stencil over the nest and stencil a few leaves and berries around the edge of the nest. Repeat on the other side of the desk.

WALL BORDER

SWAGS ARE STRONG *visual elements and must be evenly spaced in relation to a room's dimensions, doors, windows, and decorative components. Use deeper coloring on the thin parts of the ribbons and the lower edges of the ivy leaves. Follow steps 1–4 for the wall border on page 23. Substitute the ivy-swag on page 91 in step 2. Use the photo above as a guide to color placement. Once you have painted the swags, add the bird and chick and bird nest and eggs (page 91).*

TIP

A large swag requires careful planning. To help in placing your designs, make several photocopies of the design and tape them around the room to check placement.

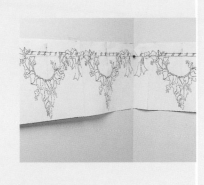

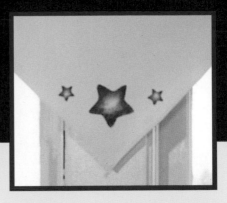

T*he focal point of this collection is a nautical bed that I stenciled for our beach house. To complement the bed, I stenciled a few boats randomly on the wall and made a coordinating lampshade and window valance. Complete instructions are given for the bed. The lampshade, window valance, and wall designs are easy adaptations made with stencils from the collection.*

I STENCILED *the rope-and-ship design on the headboard and footboard of the bed to complement a sailboat quilt I had made for the bed earlier.*

MATERIALS

+ Nautical stencil designs as listed at right
+ Acetate or card-stock paper
+ Spray adhesive
+ Pen
+ Stencil paint in light brown, tan, cobalt, medium blue, red, off-white, light blue
+ Palette
+ Brushes
+ Paper towels
+ Pencil

INSTRUCTIONS

NOTE: *Refer to the general instructions for "Applying the Paint" on pages 12–14.*

1. Use the designs on pages 92 and 93 to make stencils of the rope oval and ship. Follow the instructions for "Making Your Own Stencils" on pages 10–11.

2. Apply spray adhesive to the back of the rope oval; allow to dry for about 5 minutes. Press the stencil onto the center of the headboard, aligning the center marks on the stencil with the center of the bed. Draw a line on the outside edge of the rope. Rotate the stencil and repeat for the remaining half of the oval. Remove the stencil.

3. Paint the oval using light blue paint and a large stencil brush. Allow to dry.

4. Place the rope stencil back into postition over the blue oval and stencil over the window openings with light brown paint. Rotate the stencil and repeat for the remaining half of the oval.

5. Using a stencil brush, pounce medium blue paint onto the lower one-third of the oval inside the rope design. Pounce clouds in a random pattern onto the upper two-thirds of the oval using off-white paint.

6. Stencil the ship in the center of the rope oval, stenciling each color separately. If you like, add detail to the sails with a felt-tip pen.

7. Stencil the ship motif on the center front of the footboard in the same manner as the headboard.

VALANCE

WHAT A HAPPY *discovery to realize that simply draping a few stenciled napkins over a rod will create a valance. Stencil the large and small stars (pages 92–93) on the corner of each napkin; then fold them carefully over a curtain rod for an easy window treatment.*

LAMPSHADE

TO MAKE THE *lampshade, follow the basic instructions for the ribbons and flowers lampshade on page 33 and substitute the small star on page 92.*

WALL DESIGN

USE THE BOAT *design on page 92 to stencil the walls. Space the boats evenly in a random pattern. Read over the instructions on page 52 for general information about stenciling a wall design.*

WAVE COLLECTION

Although the techniques for decorating floors with stencil designs are the same as for walls and furniture, the preparation and finishing for floors must be more thorough. The natural grain of wood and the pebbling of cork add a richness and depth to stenciling.

Design your floor stencils to work with the existing features of the room as a whole. Take the colors, proportions, and other design elements in the room into account. You can stencil on bare, stained, or painted wood, or cork. If you are working on an old floor, clean the floor thoroughly to remove any wax, polish, or dirt. Ventilate the room and use cloths dampened with paint thinner or turpentine to remove waxes and oils. Since floor finishes must be very durable, plan to cover the floor with a protective coating at the end of the stenciling process. The newer polyurethane seals are the most durable floor finishes and do not yellow the wood or the designs.

The stencil on the beach house living room floor has the look of a large S consisting of streaks and splashes of water. The design covers the space of two cork tiles and runs as a border around the outer edges of the room. Since the lines separating the tiles are already in place permanently, the stenciling process is really quite simple. I left the outermost tile around the outer edges of the room unstenciled and painted the second row of tiles around the perimeter of the room. To complement the floor design, I stenciled an easy valance to match. Complete instructions are given for stenciling the floor and valance.

MATERIALS

+ Chalk
+ Stencil designs as listed below
+ Acetate or card-stock paper
+ Spray adhesive
+ Stencil paint in cobalt blue and medium blue
+ Palette
+ Brushes
+ Paper towels
+ Satin-finish polyurethane

INSTRUCTIONS

NOTE: *Refer to the general instructions for "Applying the Paint" on pages 12–14.*

1. With chalk, mark an outline of the tiles to be stenciled. If it is possible, plan to complete an S-shaped wave before turning the corner and start the next S after the corner. If the room has many nooks and crannies, try to simplify the stencil border so that there are not too many corners to turn. In some cases it might be necessary to leave a border of 2 unstenciled squares at one end of the room.

2. Use the wave design on page 94 to make a stencil. Follow the instructions for "Making Your Own Stencils" on pages 10–11. I cut a separate stencil for each paint color.

3. Apply spray adhesive to the back of the stencil; allow to dry for about 5 minutes. Stencil the wave pattern on the floor using 1 stencil and paint color. Lift and move the stencil as necessary to complete the entire border. Allow the paint to dry before laying down the second stencil.

4. Stencil with the second paint color, carefully aligning the stencil with the first painted image so the colors don't overlap. Allow to dry thoroughly.

5. Coat the floor with 3 or 4 thin coats of satin-finish polyurethane.

VALANCE

This simple valance *is made from a rectangle of fabric that has been stapled to a board and mounted above the window frame. The valance shown hangs 9" long. It is mounted to the wall using angle irons and screws. If the angle irons are mounted between wall studs, be sure to use the proper plastic anchors or toggles to hold the window treatment in place.*

MATERIALS

+ Metal measuring tape
+ Mounting board ¾" x 2½" x desired length
+ Saw
+ Fabric
+ Sewing machine and general sewing tools
+ Thread to match fabric
+ Iron and ironing board
+ Chalk pencil
+ Acetate or card-stock paper
+ Stencil design as listed below
+ Spray adhesive
+ Stencil paint in cobalt blue and medium blue
+ Palette
+ Brushes
+ Paper towels
+ Staple gun and staples
+ Two 2" angle irons and screws
+ Plastic anchors or toggles, if necessary

INSTRUCTIONS

NOTE: *Refer to the general instructions for "Applying the Paint" on pages 12–14.*

1. Measure the width of the window, including any window frame, and add 4". Cut your mounting board to this length. Take this measurement and add 25" to determine the length of fabric to cut. This measurement allows for a 12" drop on each side, and ½" seam allowances. For a 9" long valance with self-fabric lining, cut the fabric 24" wide. This allows for the length of the valance (9") plus the width of the board (2½") plus ½" for the seam allowance on one long side. When multiplied by 2 to allow for the lining, the total is 24". Cut a fabric rectangle to the determined measurements.

2. Fold the fabric rectangle in half, right sides together. Stitch ½" from the raw edges, leaving an opening on the long side for turning. Trim the seam allowances. Turn right side out; press. Turn in raw edges at opening; press. Mark a line 2½" from the long seamed edge.

3. Use the wave design on page 94 to make a stencil. Follow the instructions for "Making Your Own Stencils" on pages 10–11. I cut a separate stencil for each paint color. Mark the center of the long fabric edges with pins.

4. Apply spray adhesive to the back of the first stencil; allow to dry for about 5 minutes. Place the stencil to the right or left of the marked center. Stencil the wave pattern on the valance, centered between the chalk line and the lower edge of the fabric. Repeat the stenciling along the length of the fabric, spacing as desired. End the pattern with a complete design, allowing excess fabric at the ends to be unstenciled, if necessary. Allow the paint to dry before laying down the second stencil.

5. Stencil with the second paint color, carefully aligning the stencil with the first painted image so the colors don't overlap. Allow to dry thoroughly.

6. Mark the center of the mounting board. Place the seamed edge of the valance along the edge of the mounting board and the chalk line at the edge of the board on the other side; match the center of the valance with the center of the board. Staple the valance to the board along the seamed edge.

7. Attach the angle irons to each end of the mounting board on the underside with screws. Mount the valance to the wall, centered above the window.

These whimsical coffeepots and cups are perfect for a lively kitchen. The wall quilt adds a splash of color to the room. Each block has only four brightly colored pieces surrounding an easily stenciled center. The slight tilt of the coffee cups and pots gives the quilt a quirky, joyful feeling. Consider other kitchen coordinates such as a tablecloth, apron, or tea towels stenciled with one to three motifs. You could even decide to make these coffee-pots and cups dance around the room as a wall border.

WALL QUILT

This bright, cheery *quilt symbolizes all the camaraderie and liveliness of the traditional coffee break. Each block measures 8½" square and the finished quilt measures 43" square.*

NOTE: *For detailed instructions on making a quilt, refer to* The Joy of Quilting, *Joan Hanson and Mary Hickey, That Patchwork Place, Bothell, Wash., 1995.*

MATERIALS

44"-wide fabric. Prewash all fabrics.

+ A and B patterns
+ 1 yd. muslin
+ ¼ yd. or scraps of red, yellow, blue, and green fabric for piecing (I used both a dark and medium value of each color.)
+ ¼ yd. yellow fabric for inner border
+ ½ yd. blue fabric for outer border
+ ⅛ yd. fabric for binding
+ Iron and ironing board
+ Stencil designs as listed below
+ Acetate or card-stock paper
+ Stencil paint in red, blue, green, and gold
+ Palette
+ Brushes
+ Paper towels
+ Sewing machine and general sewing tools
+ 1½ yds. quilt batting
+ 1½ yds. fabric for backing

INSTRUCTIONS
Cutting

1. Use piece B (page 69) to cut sixteen 6¾" squares from the muslin.

2. Use piece A (page 69) to cut 16 triangles of each of the 4 colored fabrics. Notice that in the sample I used 8 fabrics, a medium and a dark shade of 4 colors.

3. Cut 4 strips of yellow fabric measuring 2" x 36" for the inner border.

4. Cut 4 strips of blue fabric measuring 3¾" x 45" for the outer border.

5. From the binding fabric, cut and piece 200" of 2½"-wide strips for the binding.

Stenciling the Quilt Blocks

1. Fold 12 of the squares of muslin in half on the diagonal and press a crease. Use the crease to help you position the stencils over the muslin squares.

2. Use the designs on page 82 and 95 to make stencils of the strawberry and flower, coffeepot, and coffee cup. Follow the instructions for "Making Your Own Stencils" on pages 10–11.

3. Stencil 4 coffeepots on muslin squares, placing the motifs upright and slightly tilted on the pressed diagonal lines. Reverse the stencil for 2 of the coffeepots. Stencil the lids in contrasting colors.

4. Stencil 2 coffee cups in each color on muslin squares, reversing some of them. Stencil the steam mark above the cup.

5. Fold 4 of the muslin squares in half along the straight grain of the fabric and press a crease.

6. Stencil 1 coffee cup in each color on the muslin squares from step 5. Use the fold to help you position the stencil over the straight grain.

7. Stencil the strawberry and flower as desired on the center of each cup and coffeepot.

Sewing

1. Stitch a blue triangle to the top of each stenciled square and stitch a green triangle to the bottom of each stenciled square.

2. Stitch a yellow triangle to the right of each stenciled square and stitch a red triangle to the left of each stenciled square.

3. Arrange the blocks into 4 rows of 4 blocks with 3 cups and 1 coffeepot in each row.

4. Stitch the blocks into 4 rows. Stitch the rows together to form the quilt top.

5. Sew the yellow inner border to the quilt top; miter the corners.

6. Sew the blue outer border to the quilt top.

7. Layer the quilt top with batting and backing; baste.

8. Hand or machine quilt in the design of your choice.

9. Bind the quilt edges.

8½" finished block

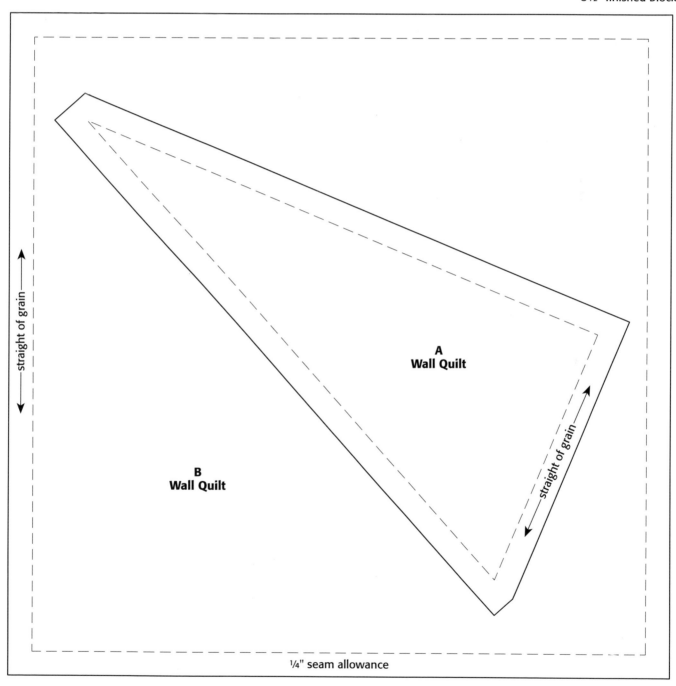

straight of grain

A
Wall Quilt

B
Wall Quilt

straight of grain

¼" seam allowance

Connect design along this line.

Connect design along this line.

Bird Collection
Quit Blocks
Enlarge all designs on this page 200%.

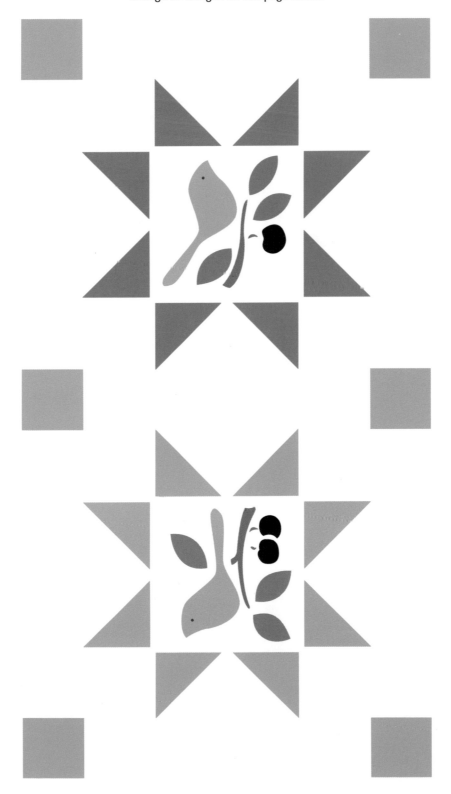

Bird Collection
Birds on Twigs
Enlarge designs on this page 125%.

Sun, Moon, and Stars Collection
Crescent
Enlarge design 200%.

Sun, Moon, and Stars Collection
Sun Rays
Enlarge design 200%.

Sun, Moon, and Stars Collection
Star 2
Full-size design

Sun, Moon, and Stars Collection
Star 1
Full-size design

Sun, Moon, and Stars Collection
Star 4
Full-size design

Sun, Moon, and Stars Collection
Star 5
Full-size design

Sun, Moon, and Stars Collection
Star 3
Full-size design

Sun, Moon, and Stars Collection
Small Moon
Full-size design
Large Moon
Enlarge design 200%.

Sun, Moon, and Stars Collection
Sun Face
Enlarge design 200%.

Ribbons and Flowers Collection
Flower Cluster 2
Full-size design

Ribbons and Flowers Collection
Large Ribbon-and-Flower Swag
Enlarge design 250%.

Ribbons and Flowers Collection
Flower Cluster 1
Full-size design

Ribbons and Flowers Collection
Ribbon Garland
Enlarge design 200%.

Ribbons and Flowers Collection
Small Ribbon-and-Flower Swag
Enlarge design 200%.

Ribbon tails for →
dresser apron

Repeat design along this line.

Raspberries Collection
Bird 3
Full-size design

Raspberries Collection/
Blue Dish Collection
Border
Full-size design

Raspberries Collection
Bird 2
Full-size design

Raspberries Collection
Wall and Cornice Border
Enlarge design 200%.

Raspberries Collection/
Blue Dish Collection
Raspberry Cluster 2
Full-size design

Raspberry Collection
Bird 1
Full-size design

Blue Dish Collection
Ivy Swags and Bird Collection
Twisted Ribbon
Full-size design

Blue Dish Collection
Bluebird and Flower
Full-size design

Blue Dish Collection
Cup 1
Full-size design

Blue Dish Collection
Strawberries
Full-size design

Blue Dish Collection
Scalloped Border
Full-size design

Blue Dish Collection
Border
Full-size design

Blue Dish Collection
Creamer 1
Full-size design

Blue Dish Collection
Cup 2
Full-size design

Blue Dish Collection
Cup 3
Full-size design

Blue Dish Collection
Creamer 2
Full-size design

Blue Dish Collection
Floral Cluster
Full-size design

Blue Dish Collection
Teapot 1 (Interior)
Enlarge design 125%.

Blue Dish Collection
Pitcher
Enlarge design 200%.

Blue Dish Collection
Teapot 1
Enlarge design 125%.

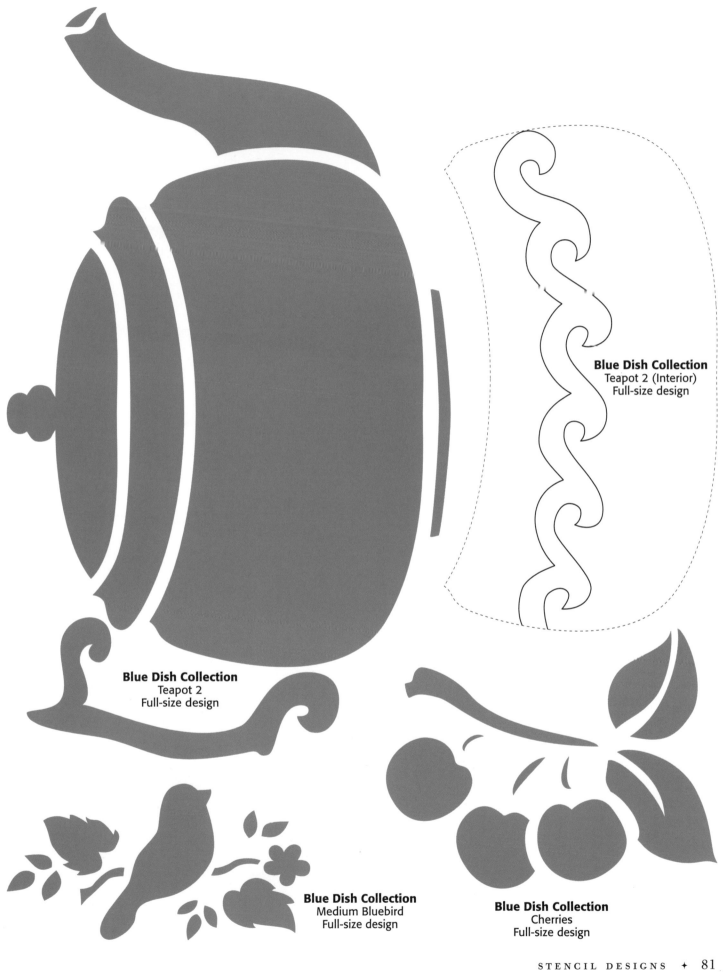

Blue Dish Collection
Teapot 2 (Interior)
Full-size design

Blue Dish Collection
Teapot 2
Full-size design

Blue Dish Collection
Medium Bluebird
Full-size design

Blue Dish Collection
Cherries
Full-size design

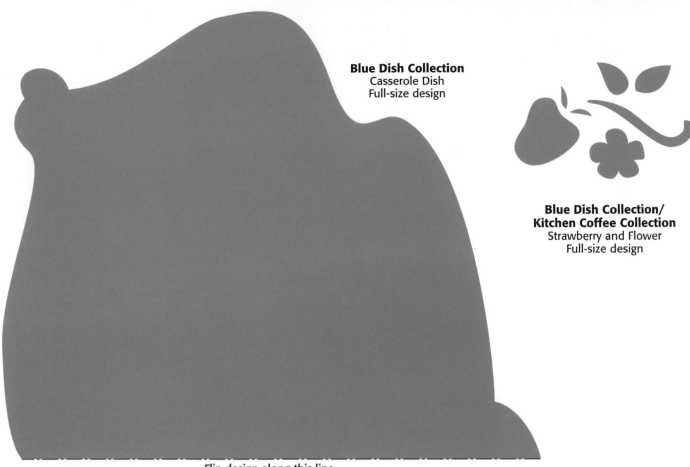

Blue Dish Collection
Casserole Dish
Full-size design

**Blue Dish Collection/
Kitchen Coffee Collection**
Strawberry and Flower
Full-size design

Flip design along this line.

Blue Dish Collection
Small Bluebird
Full-size design

Blue Dish Collection
Casserole Dish (Interior)
Full-size design

Flip design along this line.

Blue Dish Collection
Large Bluebird
Full-size design

Blue Dish Collection
Cup 4
Full-size design

Blue Dish Collection
Plate
Enlarge design 125%.

Blue Dish Collection
Floral Bouquet
Full-size design

Blue Dish Collection
Eyelet Shelf Edging
Full-size design

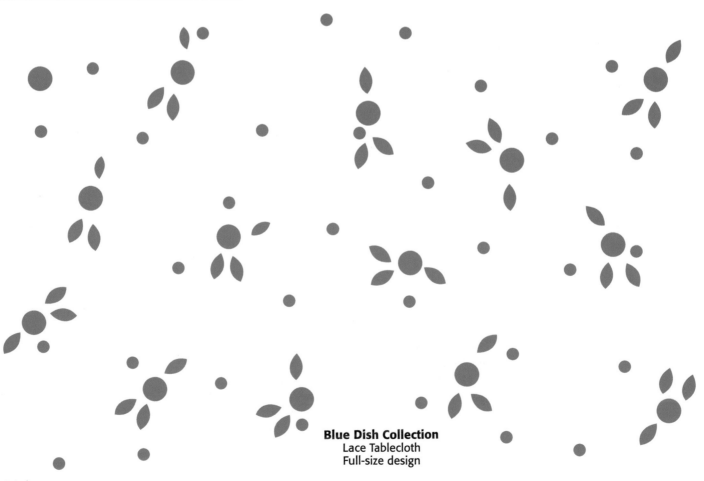

Blue Dish Collection
Lace Tablecloth
Full-size design

Blue Dish Collection
Teapot 3
Full-size design

Raspberries Collection/
Blue Dish Collection
Raspberry Cluster 1
Full-size design

Oak Leaf and Acorn Collection
Oak-Leaf Swag
Full-size design

**Oak Leaf and
Acorn Collection**
Flower Border
Full-size design

Oak Leaf and Acorn Collection
Oak-Leaf Border
Enlarge design 125%.

Oak Leaf and Acorn Collection
Long Oak-Leaf Garland
Enlarge design 200%.

Oak Leaf and Acorn Collection
Short Oak-Leaf Garland
Full-size design

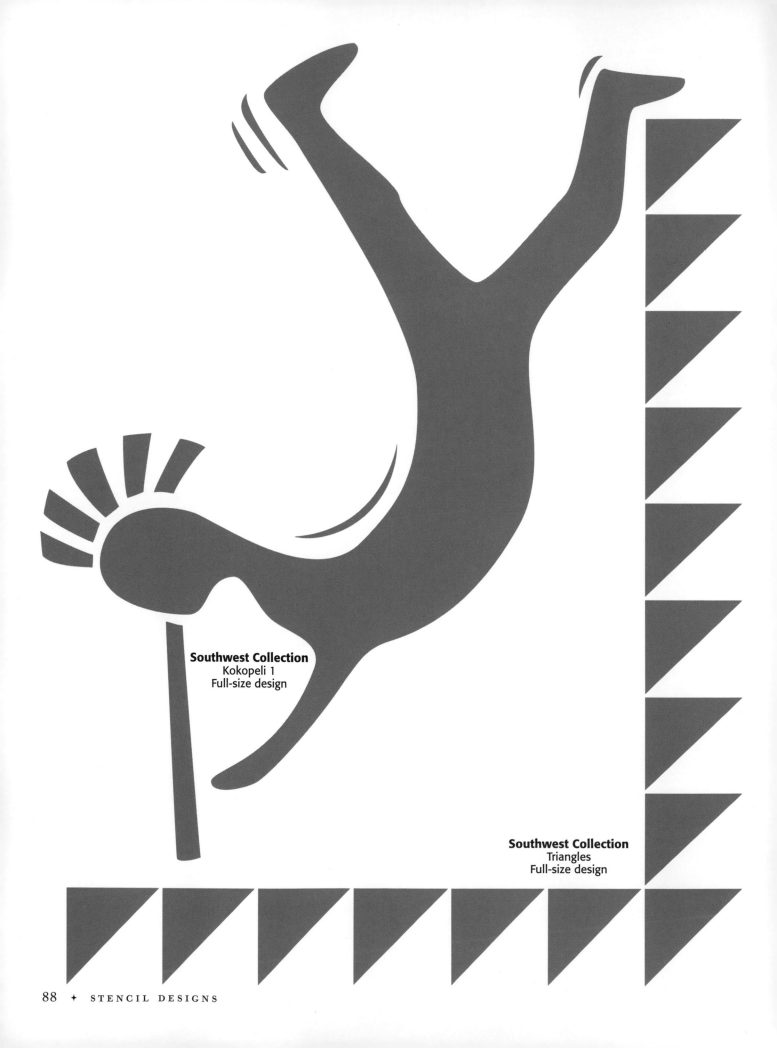

Southwest Collection
Kokopeli 1
Full-size design

Southwest Collection
Triangles
Full-size design

Southwest Collection
Kokopeli 3
Full-size design

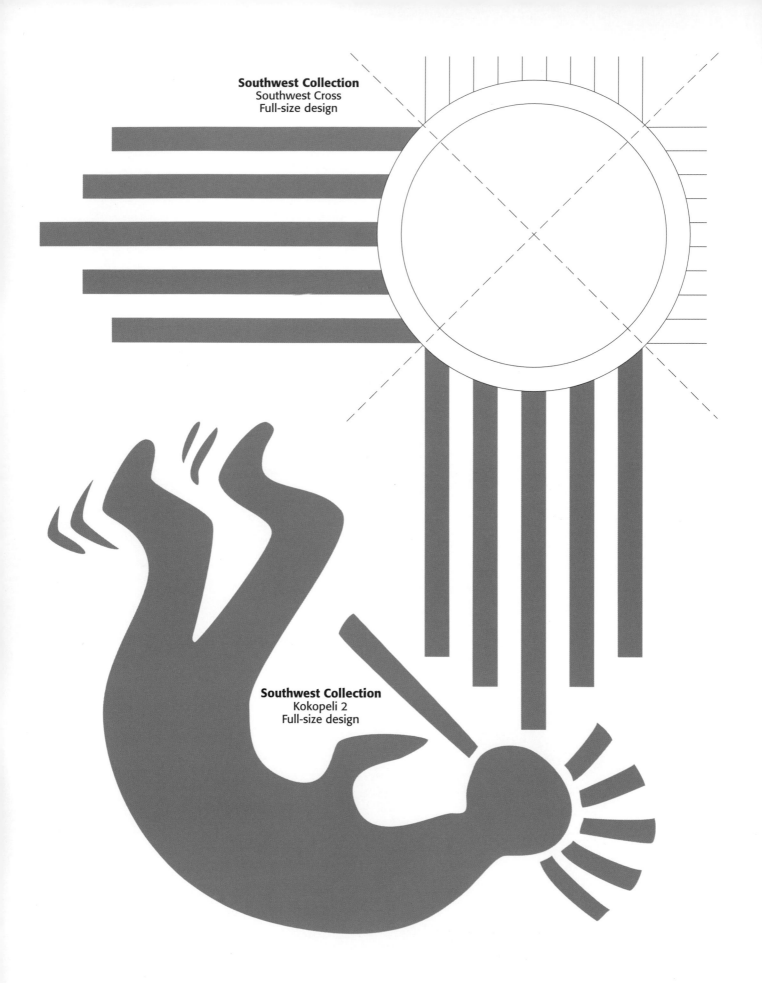

Southwest Collection
Southwest Cross
Full-size design

Southwest Collection
Kokopeli 2
Full-size design

Ivy Swags and Bird Collection
Bird Nest and Eggs
Full-size design

Ivy Swags and Bird Collection
Birds in Nest
Full-size design

**Ivy Swags and
Bird Collection**
Ivy Swag
Enlarge design 200%.

Ivy Swags and Bird Collection
Bird and Chick
Full-size design

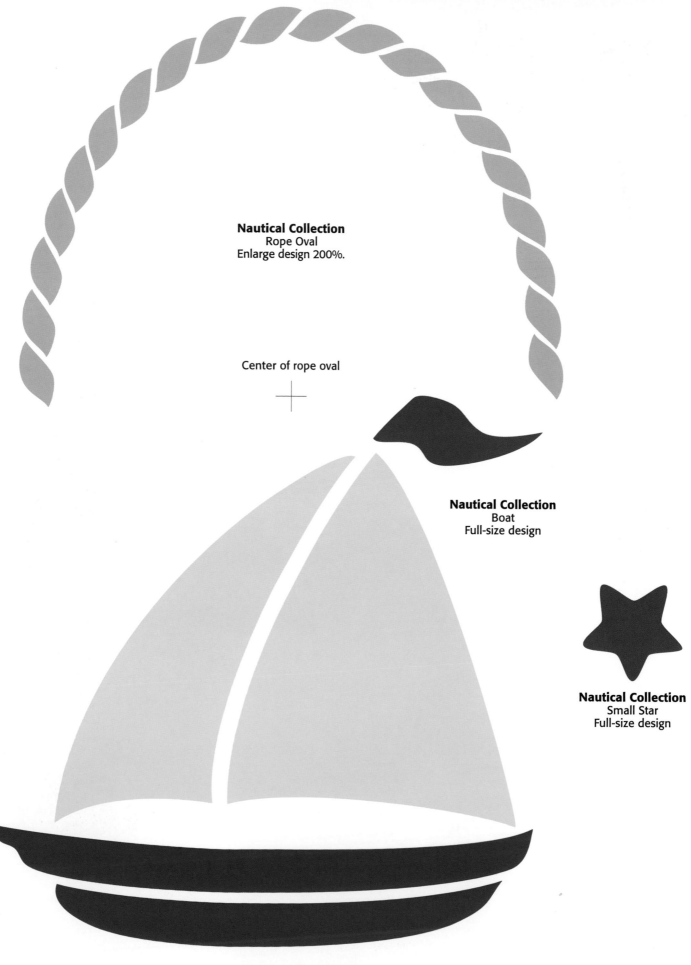

Nautical Collection
Rope Oval
Enlarge design 200%.

Center of rope oval

Nautical Collection
Boat
Full-size design

Nautical Collection
Small Star
Full-size design

Nautical Collection
Large Star
Full-size design

Nautical Collection
Ship
Enlarge design 125%.

Wave Collection
Wave
Enlarge design 200%.

Kitchen Coffee Collection
Coffee Cup
Full-size design

Kitchen Coffee Collection
Coffeepot
Full-size design

MARY HICKEY is an enthusiastic designer of stencils, fabrics, and quilts. She has traveled all around the world meeting wonderful fellow artists and quiltmakers while teaching classes in quilting and basic design. In Africa she had students come to class carrying sewing machines on their heads, and in Alaska she taught classes in the local fish cannery. Everywhere and with all groups of people, Mary's message is the same: All women are creative and place their touch and spirit on their homes and workplaces. Mary's greatest joy is in encouraging the creative abilities of each woman and bolstering the confidence of each student.

Mary and her husband, Phil, live on Liberty Bay just west of Seattle, Washington. No piece of furniture or wall is ever really safe from Mary's paintbrush. However, her young-adult children, Maureen, Josh, and Molly, frequently offer to find space in their homes for Mary's creations, both furniture and quilts. Mary has written several quilting books: *Little by Little, Basket Garden, Angle Antics, Pioneer Storybook Quilts,* and *The Big Book of Small Quilts,* and co-authored *Quick and Easy Quiltmaking* and *The Joy of Quilting.* Mary also designs fabric for quilts and feels very lucky to be able to do all of these activities and call them work when they are so much fun.